THE EAST END AT WORK

A working girl – Ada Reeve, music-hall star, *c.* 1900. Born Adelaide Mary Isaacs in Jubilee Street, Stepney, on 3 March 1874, she was the eldest of sixteen children whose parents were members of a touring theatrical company. Her first appearance on stage was at the age of four, at the Pavilion Theatre, Whitechapel. She began her music-hall career at Sebrights Music Hall in 1886, and in 1899 was top of the bill at the Lyric Theatre in *Florodora*. Her stage experience covered the Edwardian music hall, burlesque, Shakespeare, film, radio and television. Ada Reeve continued to appear on stage and television when she was well into her eighties. She died, aged ninety-two, on 26 September 1966.

BRITAIN IN OLD PHOTOGRAPHS

THE EAST END AT WORK

ROSEMARY TAYLOR AND
CHRISTOPHER LLOYD

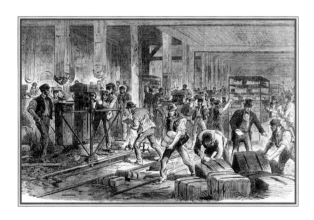

TOWER HAMLETS LOCAL HISTORY LIBRARY
SUTTON PUBLISHING LIMITED

Sutton Publishing Limited
Phoenix Mill · Thrupp · Stroud
Gloucestershire · GL5 2BU

First published 1999

Title page picture: Globe Wharf, Regents
Canal, Mile End Road, 1867. Workers
at the firm of Edward John Davis, Hay
Pressers, preparing compressed forage at
the wharf. Hay was sold at the hay market
in Whitechapel High Street until 1928.
Globe Wharf was situated on the south
side of Mile End Road, on the west bank
of Regent's Canal.

British Library Cataloguing in Publication Data
A catalogue record for this book is available from the
British Library.

ISBN 0-7509-2006-8

Typeset in 10.5/13.5 Photina.
Typesetting and origination by
Sutton Publishing Limited.
Printed in Great Britain by
Ebenezer Baylis, Worcester.

CONTENTS

INTRODUCTION

The photographs chosen for this book depict the area which is now the London Borough of Tower Hamlets. The borough was created in 1965 through the amalgamation of the Metropolitan Boroughs of Stepney, Bethnal Green and Poplar, which were themselves formed in 1900 out of the parishes and hamlets of Stepney, St George's in the East, Mile End Old Town, Shadwell, Ratcliffe, Limehouse, Poplar, Bethnal Green, Spitalfields, Whitechapel, Bow and Bromley.

In the eighteenth century and earlier the area was considered an idyllic rural retreat from the grimy, smoky City of London, where gentle folk came to breathe the fresh country air. The hamlets of east London gradually began to attract the small traders, the merchants and the craftsmen eager to sell their wares to the prosperous City dwellers. Unable to ply their trade in the City itself, where the Guilds controlled all trade and commerce, the 'foreigners' were forced to set up their businesses beyond the confines of the City of London. Stepney shared its boundary with the City of London along its western edge and much of its early industry was an overspill from the City. The Rag Fairs at Wapping and Houndsditch, the weavers in Spitalfields and Bethnal Green, the fruit and vegetable market in Spitalfields, the hay market at Whitechapel, the brewers of ale in Stepney, the sugar bakers, the matchmakers, the ropemakers and the ship and boatbuilders and repairers of Poplar and Limehouse, all these and more were providers to the City. Stepney also had the largest concentration of dairymen and cowkeepers in London, providing fresh milk twice a day to thousands who could only afford to buy their daily requirement. Wapping and Ratcliffe were thriving maritime communities servicing the ships entering and leaving the Port of London and lightermen and watermen plying their trade along the Thames.

Poplar, from time immemorial, has been associated with ships and shipbuilding, the docks and the East and West India Companies. Much of Poplar, Blackwall and adjacent parts of Limehouse's economy was bound up with ships and shipbuilding from at least the fifteenth century onwards, and during the eighteenth and nineteenth centuries shipbuilding along this section of the Thames was at its zenith. Among the listed occupations in the mid-nineteenth century we find shipbuilders, shipwrights, mariners, ship's chandlers, sawyers, coopers, carpenters, painters, boatbuilders, bargebuilders, ropemakers, mastmakers, watermen and victuallers.

With the building of the docks from 1800 onwards – first the West India Docks, and then the East India Docks – the whole area experienced a rapid increase in population. The coming of the railway to Blackwall in 1840, making access to and from Fenchurch Street swift and easy, also served to accelerate the pace of growth.

Joel Gascoigne's map of 1703 shows Bethnal Green as a pleasant village surrounded by market gardens and fields. It differed from Poplar and Stepney in that it had no river frontage and did not directly serve the maritime trade and industry. Furniture, clothing manufacturers and the brewing industry were the largest employers. The Industrial Revolution, the invention of machinery to do the work that craftsmen laboured over, the factories that sprang up to cater for an ever-demanding consumer, all served to accelerate the change of pace from pleasant countryside to densely populated industrial landscape.

The transformation from a rural retreat to a place overcrowded East End dwellings began with the influx of the Huguenots from the continent. The craft of weaving was well established in Bethnal Green by the reign of Elizabeth I when silkweavers settled here – the Queen was one of the first to sport silk stockings, which were considered a scandalous luxury. When the Huguenot silkweavers emigrated to England in 1685, they came to Bethnal Green and settled here in their thousands. Two centuries later, the pogroms in Europe led to Jews fleeing Russia and Poland. They found a haven in the East End and Bethnal Green saw a dramatic increase in its population, as more and more Jews set up their businesses, factories and shops in the area.

The River Lea and the construction of the Regent's Canal and Duckett's Canal in the 1830s attracted major industries, which used them as a convenient source of water. Soap factories, paper factories, flour mills, confectionery and jam factories and breweries lined the banks of these waterways, and polluted them with their effluents. In 1884, William Bryan of Old Ford complained about the dreadful stench emanating from 'chemical and soap works, bone manure works, huge piggeries and places where condemned meat and offal are boiled in open vats. These noxious fumes are turned out in large quantities, not only in the daytime but after 10 pm and on Sunday evenings.' Summertime in Old Ford and Bow was intolerable, he said, especially when the wind was from the east.

The dramatic increase in population inevitably led to tensions within the community, as people struggled to earn a living. The docks attracted a large labour force, as there was work to be had with the daily loading and unloading of vessels calling from all parts of the world. However, work was generally of a casual nature, and men had to turn up each morning to await the call-up, hoping to catch the foreman's eye, a chance of a ticket and a day's wages. Furious scenes of savagery were witnessed at the dock gates as men fought one another for the possession of a tally. Failure meant no work and no wage, and a day without food for the family. The traditional family ideal of husband as wage earner, with the woman as homemaker, wife and mother, dependent on her father and later her husband for financial support, did not appear to be the norm in the East End. The end of the nineteenth century saw a decline in the shipbuilding industry in Poplar, and while there was work to be found in the docks, this was a time of high male unemployment, and women took whatever work they could get. A woman who struggled through long hours of work in order to pay the rent and buy a few necessities, would often go without so that her husband and children could eat. Ultimately, she paid the price for her self-neglect. Premature death from starvation was commonly recorded as the cause of death.

Margaret Harkness, who carried out extensive research into conditions among women in the East End of London, found that women were at work in at least 200 trades. They were: 'Brush-makers, button-makers, cigarette-makers, electric light fitters, fur workers, India rubber stamp machinists, magic lantern slide makers, perfumers, portmanteau makers, spectacle makers, surgical instrument makers, tie makers etc. These girls can be roughly divided into two classes: those who earn from 8s (40p) to 14s (70p), and those who earn from 4s (20p) to 8s (40p) a week.' While wages were low, the hours worked were long, the average working day being from 8 a.m. to 7 p.m., with an hour off for dinner and a half day on Saturday. Overtime meant working until 10 or 11 at night, or even throughout the night.

Besides those who worked in the factories and manufacturing businesses, or as homeworkers in the East End, there were those who earned a livelihood plying their trade through the streets and from door to door. The street seller was a familiar sight even in the post-war era. The catsmeat seller, the bagel seller, ice-cream seller, the toffee man, the muffin man, the rag-and-bone man, the shoe-black, the knife-grinder, these and many more were the mainstay of East End community life.

While every effort has been made to ensure our selection of pictures is as representative of the local industries as possible, in a few instances photographic evidence was not available, so trades familiar to many, such as the fur trade, the jewellery trade and the gun-making trade, all based in Whitechapel, have not been included.

Old Ford Lock on the River Lea, by Dace Road, 1966. A toll-free lock was first envisaged on this section of the Lea in 1850. Old Ford Lock was opened in 1866 to facilitate the transport of merchandise from riverside factories, the owners of which realized the advantages of transporting heavy material by barge down the river. Hundreds of thousands of tons of merchandise passed through these locks, everything from timber, stone, strawboards, building materials and coals.

CHAPTER ONE
SHIP & BOATBUILDING

A blacksmith on board ship, c. 1857.

There was little actual shipbuilding on the Thames in pre-Tudor times as most vessels were being built at the ports along the south coast. But Henry VIII wanted shipyards close to London so that he could supervise the building of his fleet, and by 1517 ships were being built at yards in Woolwich and Deptford. Limehouse yards were already engaged in ship-repairing and bargebuilding and Ratcliffe, Wapping and Blackwall shipyards were all established by the sixteenth century. Blackwall Yard, also known as the East India Yard, was founded in about 1587 and was the the largest of the private yards. It was just upstream of the entrance to the East India Docks and during 3 centuries 700 ships were built there, starting with the East Indiamen *Globe*, *Hector* and *Thomas* in 1612.

Between 1688 and 1815 England was at war for 63 years out of 127 and every private shipbuilder was kept fully occupied. Those in the Limehouse, Ratcliffe area included Grevill and Whetstone, Carter, Batson, Cox and Curling, and Hill and Mellish. About twelve big ships were built each year for the East India Company and many smaller ships for the West India trade, the Hudson's Bay Company and Arctic whaling.

The Blackwall Yard built its first steamship, the *City of Edinburgh*, 401 tons, in 1821, after which it launched as many steamers as sailing ships. Only one yard apart from Blackwall Yard went on building sailing ships: Cox and Curling of Limehouse, later known as Curling and Young or Young and Magnay, was just north of the entrance to the West India Dock basin.

William Fairbairn, a great engineer, started building in iron at Millwall in 1836, and twenty-nine ships were known to have been built by his yard before it failed in 1849 and passed to John Scott Russell. In 1850 Russell designed the sailing yacht *Titania* for Robert Stephenson and a second *Titania* for him in 1853. Scott Russell built the Australian mail steamers *Victoria* and *Adelaide* in 1852, wave-form ships designed by him to Brunel's specifications. Isambard Kingdom Brunel persuaded the Eastern Steam Navigation Co. to build the *Leviathan*, always known as the *Great Eastern*, 690 ft long, at Scott Russell's yard. After an abortive first attempt, the *Great Eastern* was launched by Brunel on 31 January 1858. Scott Russell also worked with Isaac Watt, the Surveyor of the Navy, on the *Warrior*, 9,210 tons, the first seagoing warship which from the outset carried armour and was the largest warship of her day. She was built by the Thames Iron Works at Blackwall. A fire in 1853 destroyed the yard, with damage estimated at £100,000, which was mostly covered by insurance, but the firm closed in 1861 and Scott Russell died in 1882.

In 1856 Joseph Westwood left Thames Iron Works, and with his colleagues Campbell and Baillie set up a yard on the Isle of Dogs. They built about a dozen ships, before specializing in bridge construction. They helped to build the Britannia Bridge over the Menai Straits, and also the Sukkar Bridge in Pakistan, the largest cantilever bridge of the time. At Millwall Wharf, between Dudgeon's Yard and Westwood and Baillie's premises, were the yards of Hepworth and James Ash.

In 1843 Blackwall Yard was divided, the western half becoming Money Wigram & Sons and the eastern half R. & H. Green. Richard and Henry Green built hundreds of ships, continuing their father George Green's great tradition. Three ships deserve mention: the *Challenger* in 1851, an outstanding China tea clipper, the *Amazon*, a paddle steamer of 2,256 tons for the RMSP Co., and the little paddle steamer *Duke of Devonshire* in 1896, which is now called *Cosens* and is still afloat. The yard ceased building in 1901 and later became part of R. & H. Green Silley Weir & Co.'s ship-repairing organization. Money Wigram & Sons turned to iron almost immediately and built some very successful auxiliary passenger ships which they put on to the Australia run. Their yard closed in 1876.

Fletcher & Fearnall of Limehouse built the crack opium clipper *Time*. Fletcher's Dock was made in 1818 by sinking the old East Indiaman *Canton*, the timbers forming a graving dock which was successfully used until 1898 when a more conventional type of dry dock was constructed on the site.

In 1843 Samuda Brothers opened a yard on Blackwall Reach, ½ mile north of Dudgeons at Cubitt Town. The yard built forty-nine warships and cross Channel steamers until its closure in 1891. These included warships for the German and Japanese navies.

Yarrow and Hedley began operating from Folly Yard on the Isle of Dogs in 1866. They built 350 steam launches in 7 years and in 1873 built the first of the shallow-river steamers for which they became famous. In 1875 Alfred Yarrow became sole owner of the firm and in 1876 they sold their first torpedo boat to a foreign navy. They went on to build torpedo boats for Argentina, Spain, France, Holland, Greece, Austria, Russia, Italy and Chile as well as the Royal Navy. However, Alfred Yarrow who was a tough nineteenth-century businessman, became convinced that ships could not be built economically on Thames. He closed down his yard and moved the firm to Scotstoun on the Clyde in the early 1900s.

In 1838 C.J. Mare set up at Orchard Place in Blackwall. He began to build for the P&O Company, and the *Himalaya* of 1853 was the largest merchant ship of the time. Six ships were built for the P&O and seventy-five ships in all were built before C.J. Mare & Co. became bankrupt in 1856. The Thames Iron Works was taken over by a board of directors and continued to progress. From 1857 to 1865 they built two large mail steamers for the RMSP Co. and eight for the P&O Co. After that no more liners were built on the Thames. In the same period they built the *Warrior* and *Minotaur*, armoured frigates of over 10,000 tons, and a host of other ships. In 1880 Arnold Hills joined the company and Thames Iron Works prospered for the next thirty years.

Few people know that the Thames was famous for shipbuilding, fewer still that it was a great boatbuilding centre. First Harton of Limehouse and then Forrestt's built lifeboats for the Royal National Lifeboat Institution and sent them all around the coast. But the small firm could not always carry the stocks of prime timber necessary to meet the exacting standards of the Institution. In 1895 Thames Iron Works added boatbuilding to its other activities and in 1896 they became the official builders to the RNLI; 206 lifeboats were built between 1896 and 1911.

The last of the shipbuilders suffered a fatal blow when northern firms began undercutting Thames rates. Arnold Hills suspected foul play, but, unable to prove it, the final contract was signed in 1911 when the Dreadnought *Thunderer* was built by Thames Iron Works. But by 1912 shipbuilding on the Thames had come to an end.

Manchester Road, Cubitt Town, looking north from the Queen Public House towards what is now the Blue Bridge over the entrance to the West India Docks, 1919. The houses on the left are Glen Terrace. On the right the steel sailing ship *Milverton* is under repair at John Stewart's Canal Dockyard, a rigger carefully making his way back down the bowsprit of the ship.

Captain William Harrison, commander of the *Great Eastern* steamship, 1858. Harrison joined the Great Ship Company in 1857 and was one of Brunel's most loyal supporters. In January 1860 Harrison, the nine-year-old son of the Chief Purser and the Coxswain were all drowned when the small boat in which they were attempting to get ashore overturned during a squall.

The interior of a workshop at Mare and Co.'s Iron Shipbuilding Works, Bow Creek, Blackwall, 1854. In 1838 C.J. Mare and Thomas Ditchburn set up their shipbuilding yard at Orchard Place, Blackwall. Ditchburn left in 1846, and Mare continued to build ships, especially for the P&O, but ran into difficulties and by 1856 was bankrupt. Almost immediately Mare got backing from Overend Gurney, second in importance only to the Bank of England, to re-open Scott Russell's yard as the Millwall Ironworks and Shipbuilding Co. He put £100,000 into the yard and seventeen ships were built there before HMS *Northumberland* got stuck on the slipways in 1866 while being launched. In the same year Overend Gurney went bankrupt; this financial collapse was one of the most dramatic ever to shake the City and caused the ruination of firms all over the country.

Interior of one of the tanks on board the *Great Eastern, c.* 1865. This scene below decks shows the workmen engaged in unwinding a cable.

The *Great Eastern* at Millwall, November 1857. Isambard Kingdom Brunel, the great Victorian engineer and visionary, persuaded the Eastern Steam Navigation Co. to build the *Leviathan*, 690 ft long, at Scott Russell's Millwall yard. The dimensions and specifications were Brunel's, the design Scott Russell's. She was wave-form and framed on his longitudinal system. From the outset, the two men came into conflict with each other. The *Great Eastern* was built broadside on to the river and the great length of her – she was fifteen times the size of the largest vessel then afloat – is marked on the wall today. Scott Russell would have built her stern in the usual way and he was probably right, because she immobilized the whole yard and part of the old Napier Yard next door for four years while the Eastern Steam Navigation Co. got into difficulties. This picture shows workmen checking the drums on the *Great Eastern*. Minutes after this photograph was taken the drum crew were thrown into the air and one of them was killed.

The yard at the Millwall Ironworks and Shipbuilding Co., *c.* 1883. This very early photograph shows workmen in the foreground examining planks of wood, behind them can be seen a gentleman in a top hat. This picture is unusual in that it is not a 'posed' one, so that some of the figures are blurred. Founded by William Fairbairn in 1836, who did much of the basic research on iron ships and bridges, the yard built twenty-nine ships before Fairbairn went bankrupt and was taken over by John Scott Russell, who built over thirty ships here, including the *Great Eastern*. Some of the finest of the early paddle engines were built at this yard by John Scott Russell.

Yarrow and Hedley's shipbuilding works, Isle of Dogs, *c.* 1870. Alfred Yarrow, the founder of the firm, served his apprenticeship with Ravenhill and Salkeld of Ratcliffe, located on the eastern shore of the Isle of Dogs. Yarrow and Hedley began here in 1866 and built 350 steam launches in 7 years. The firm continued building ships until Yarrow moved to Scotland in the early 1900s.

Royal National Lifeboat Institution storeyard, *c.* 1885. The storeyard opened in Broomfield Street, Poplar, in 1882 as the headquarters of the RNLI and had large storerooms with equipment to deal with the repair and maintenance of its fleet of lifeboats, as well as a reserve fleet for emergencies. It had a graving dock and slipway into Limehouse Cut, which connects the River Lea with the Thames. The steady mechanization of the fleet made it necessary for larger premises to be built at Elstree and in 1933 it was decided to close the storeyard in Poplar; the buildings were demolished in 1977.

Messrs Forrestt's lifeboat building yard, Limehouse, 17 November 1860. T. & W. Forrestt had built boats at Limehouse from 1788 to 1890, when they moved to Wivenhoe. First Harton of Limehouse and then Forrestt's built lifeboats for the Royal National Lifeboat Institution. In 1895 Arnold Hills added boatbuilding to the other activities of the Thames Ironworks and in 1896 they became the official builders to the RNLI.

Royal National Lifeboat Institution storeyard, 27 Broomfield Street, Poplar, 1923. Inside the storeyard lifeboats are being checked over. Lifeboats were sent here from all round the coast to be repaired and refitted and were then tried out in Limehouse Cut.

RNLI storeyard, 1923. Workmen are seen repairing a lifeboat. About seventy men and women were permanently employed here, repairing damaged lifeboats, among them carpenters, engineers and riggers, many of whom had been in the Royal Navy.

Fred and Albert, boatbuilders, with their mate Frank, Old Ford, *c.* 1913. This yard is the same as the picture below, which would place it at No. 87 Rippoth Road, the residence of Frederick Monksfield. The three men are all set for a trip in their boat, complete with Gladstone bags, primus stove and loaves of bread.

Fred and Albert working on their boat *Puffin* at Old Ford, *c.* 1913. Their other boat *Fury* is pulled up ahead of them. The yard was at the top end of Roach Road, by the Hertford Union (Duckett's) Canal. This photograph was used as a post card and is postmarked 21 July 1913. There is a message on the back signed Bill. This was Albert's pseudonym when he was courting Miss Jenny Scott, who was then in service at 440 Old Ford Road (Chance the baker's). Jenny and Albert married in 1920. In the background is the factory of Carless, Capel and Leonard's Pharos Works, manufacturers of naphtha, benzoline, gasolene and petrol. They were the first to use the word 'petrol' to describe the fuel produced for motor cars, but were unable to get a patent for the name.

CHAPTER TWO

WORKING IN THE DOCKS

An illustration showing dock labourers being engaged at the West India Docks, 1886. This scene was a daily occurrence for the thousands of casual dock labourers who turned up every morning, and waited on the stones to catch the foreman's eye, in the hope of getting a ticket for a day or a half day's labour.

Before the construction of London's docks, all cargo could only be offloaded at the Legal Quays. Often this took several weeks and the congestion in the Thames was considerable. So was theft, and some merchants lost up to a third of their cargo before it could be landed. There were two wet docks on the Thames, the Brunswick Dock at Blackwall and the Greenland Dock in Rotherhithe. Neither of these were allowed to act as trading docks. The Act of 1799 allowed for the construction of two dock basins in the Isle of Dogs, and in 1802 the West India Docks were opened. The high dock walls and strict security soon reduced pilferage, and in 1803, bonded warehouses were added to the system. The building of East London's dock complex from 1800 onwards attracted a large influx of labour, mainly Irish in origin, which came to build the docks, and then stayed on to work in them.

The London Docks at Wapping were constructed between 1801 and 1805, and work was slow because a large part of the site contained houses and workshops. The warehouses and vaults were the best in London, and it is still possible to admire the architecture and construction at Tobacco Dock in the Highway.

East India Company purchased the Brunswick Dock at Blackwall from Wells in 1803 and began the construction of the East India Docks. They opened for trade in 1806. Goods were not stored at Blackwall, but taken to Cutler Street warehouse. In 1834 the West India Docks took over the East India Docks and they formed a single company.

The East India Docks import dock was used during the Second World War to build the Mulberry Harbour Phoenix units, used in the D-Day landings. The dock lay derelict after the war and was then filled in and is the site of the Financial Times Press which has since closed, all printing now being done at West Ferry Printers, and the NCC buildings which contains Tower Hamlets Council offices. The export dock has been drained and is now the site of Virginia Quays, a mix of high-rise apartments and houses.

St Katharine's Dock was built in 1826–8 by Thomas Telford and caused much hardship to the local population. Some 11,300 people living in 1,250 houses were displaced and the centuries-old St Katharine's Foundation, a religious order serving the poor, was removed from the site, and relocated to Regent's Park. It is now in Butcher Row, in Ratcliff. Huge warehouses were constructed, some of which can still be seen. Millwall Docks were built to the south of the West India Docks in 1865 and opened for business in 1868, but by this time the docks were suffering a decline.

With the construction of the iron ships and steamers and bigger tonnage, there was a need for larger docks. The Royal Victoria, 1855, and the Royal Albert, 1880, further downstream, drew off a large proportion of shipping. This dock complex was further improved with the contruction from 1912–21 of the King George V Docks.

Tilbury Docks, constructed in 1882–6 contributed in no small measure to the decline of London's docks. From 1912–16 Tilbury Dock was extended for P&O berths and there were further improvements in facilities for both river- and ocean-going vessels. From the 1960s Tilbury largely superseded the old Port of London. In 1970 Tilbury opened a container service, which was improved in 1978 to accommodate large container ships. London's docks could no longer compete, and in 1980 the Royal Docks and the West India Docks closed.

Vessels in the Pool of the Thames, a nineteenth-century engraving by W. Miller, from a painting by Sir A.W. Calcott. The scene is one that would have been familiar a hundred years ago, that of watermen and wherrymen plying their trade.

The steamboat *Penchateau* discharging its cargo into a lighter in the London Docks, *c.* 1928. The *Penchateau*, ex-*Rapallo*, was built in 1920 by de Haan et Oerlemans, Hensden. It was owned by the Compagnie des Chargeurs de l'Ouest, whose headquarters were in Nantes, France. Together with their subsidiaries, the company owned about twenty tramp steamboats.

Regent's Canal Dock, Limehouse, from a watercolour by T.M. Shepperd, 1825. Lightermen are busy transporting their cargo through the basin into the Regent's Canal.

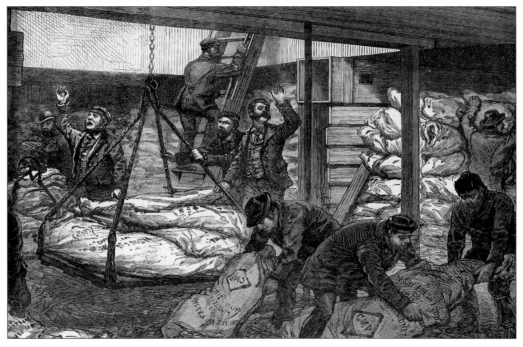

Landing Australian frozen meat from Sydney in the South West India Dock, Millwall, from the refrigerated ship *Catania*, *Illustrated London News*, 19 November 1881. The Haslam process or 'dry air refrigator' was found to be successful in the preservation and transportation of frozen meat in ships through the tropics. The *Catania* had left Sydney on 18 August and had been seventy-eight days at sea. She conveyed 1,035 quarters of Australian beef and 1,469 whole carcasses of mutton, or nearly 120 tons of meat. Each quarter of beef and each sheep was neatly tied up in white calico, which prevented ice from forming on the surface.

The SS *Cornish City* in the Royal Victoria Dock, April 1926. The grain elevator is shown discharging 7,048 tons of grain into barges, a process which took twenty-eight working hours.

Landing foreign cattle at the British and Foreign Wharf, near the London Docks, 26 August 1865. Cattle of all description were imported from Holland and Germany for the London markets, and came via Harwich and the Great Eastern Railway, as well as to Brown's Wharf at Blackwall and the Brunswick Cattle Wharf, Blackwall. The illustration shows the process of unloading a mixed cargo of sheep and cattle from the *Magnet*, a regular cattle ship. There were 1,600 sheep on the upper deck, and in the lower hold were a number of cattle, covered in sheep's droppings. The drovers got the animals off the ship on to the wharves, where they were inspected by veterinary surgeons appointed by the Board of Trade. The animals were killed in slaughterhouses attached to each wharf. The carcasses were again inspected as they entered the market in the Caledonian Road, where they were then bought by butchers.

Nutmegs in the warehouse at the London Docks, 1920. The nutmegs are being separated from their outer husk (mace) by the men hard at work in the background.

Australian dried fruit in storage at C Warehouse, St Katharine's Dock, June 1927. The workmen lined up with their barrows appear to be awaiting starter's orders! The name on the cases reads 'Moreton Bay'.

Sugar warehouses at the West India Docks, *c.* 1900. This view of South Quay, looking northwards is still recognizable today, with the Ledger House in the distance. Huge barrels containing molasses have been offloaded ready to be stored in the extensive warehouses. Barrels of rum were also stored here, and there was a constant danger of fire. The warehouses were heavily bombed during the Second World War, and the surviving block is presently being refurbished to contain luxury apartments, restaurants and cinemas.

Poplar Rum Quay, West India Docks on fire, 29 November 1933. Firemen are trying to control the blaze at the rum quay, where 3 million gallons of rum were stored; much of it was destroyed. The conflagration was so intense that firemen were still at work on the second day after the disaster. The quay caught fire at about 10 p.m. on 21 April and the area, burning furiously, was visible 25 miles away, with flames shooting up 200 ft into the air. The rum was stored in barrels and underground vaults, mostly 20 ft below water level, where it was being kept in bond by the Customs authorities. Of more than 3 million gallons stored at the quay, about 1 million, it was believed, were destroyed in the fire, representing a loss in potential duty to the Customs of about £3,750,000 which would have been gradually collected as the liquor was bought by dealers. The cause of the outbreak was unknown, but the police were investigating the possibility of an arson attack or sabotage. The precautions taken against fire were so elaborate that the possibility of an accident seems remote. At one time there were between fifty and sixty fire engines fighting the blaze.

His Majesty's Customs and Excise men checking whisky at the bonded warehouse in London Docks, 1920. Warehousemen in the background are rolling the barrels back on to the stockpile; the inspector samples the barrel in the foreground.

Unloading teaships in the East India Docks, the *Illustrated London News*, 26 October 1862. The report reads: 'We have noticed the competition between the owners of fast-sailing vessels employed in the China tea trade for the honour of bringing to the port of London the first cargo that arrives here of the freshly gathered crop of tea, which is always plucked in the spring season. The market in Mincing Lane is very busy in this month of October with the "New Season Teas" both those of China and those of the Himalayan provinces of India, which have latterly found favour. The unloading of the teaships and warehousing of their cargoes on the wharves of the East India Docks is also a scene of great activity, as shown in one of our illustrations.' The scene shows the foreman, centre front, urging the men into action. In the right background can be seen a gentleman in top hat, presumably the owner of the shipment.

Landing gold from the *Australian* steamship in the East India Docks, Blackwall, 22 January 1853. The *Australian* screw-steamer arrived with her valuable freight at Blackwall, and was immediately boarded by Superintendent Evans of the Thames Police and a party of police constables who positioned themselves on the deck and also by the side of the vessel, a mounted escort being stationed outside the dock gates. The gold was deposited in two covered waggons and left the dock for the Bank of England under an escort of mounted police commanded by Superintendent Steed of the H and Superintendent Howie of the K Divisions. When opposite Limehouse church, the off-side wheel of one of the waggons came off and caused a delay of three-quarters of an hour. The wheel having been replaced, the waggons again proceeded, amidst the cheers of the crowd, and arrived safely at the Bank of England. The *Australian* also brought the Victoria Nugget (328 ounces weight), presented to Queen Victoria by the government of Melbourne. It was found between 3 and 4 ft from the surface in the Bendigo Creek Diggings, Mount Alexander, about 90 miles from Melbourne, by Mr Barrow. It was sold by auction to the Australian government by Messrs W.M. Tennant and Co. on 23 September.

His Excellency, the Ambassador of Burma, U Hla Maug, left, standing on the biggest teak log exported from the Burma forests, January 1964. It arrived at W.W. Howard Bros Offices, Commercial Wharf Poplar, and was 750 years old, 33 ft in length, 18 ft wide and weighed 17 tonnes.

Ivory Warehouse at London Docks, 1920. Thousands of tusks lie here awaiting inspection before being bought by manufacturers of brushes, pianos, jewellery and curios.

Workers in the East India Dock Road during the Dock Strike, 1889. The Strike, popularly known as 'The Docker's Tanner Strike', heralded a new era in the history of labour unions. The dock labourers, led by Ben Tillet and others, were given encouragement to press for an increase in wages, a basic rate of a tanner (sixpence) an hour, by the example of Annie Besant, who organized the first successful strike by working women and led by a woman in the previous year at the Bryant and May Match Factory in Fairfield Road, Bow.

Workers in the docks, 1902. Entitled 'Eager for Work', the scene is one of increasing desperation as the men press against the ropes, hoping to catch the ganger's eye as he moves along distributing tickets, which meant work for the day and often the difference between food on the table and a starving family.

Troops marching down East India Dock Road during the General Strike, 1926. Soldiers were sent in to help unload cargo in the docks when the dockers went on strike. The soldiers are seen in the vicinity of Poplar Pavilion Theatre.

A 'clipper' on the Blackwall Railway at work. Because of the danger of fire in the docks, the train had no engine, the carriages being pulled along by a rope on each line of the Blackwall Railway, attached at either end to an immense drum, worked by stationary steam engines. Each rope was used alternately for up and down trains. The rope of an approaching train, after passing over the numerous stationary drums on the line, crossed an open space immediately in front of the winding drum and beneath this opening, with the carriages passing above his head, stood the 'clipper' working a huge pair of shears to guide the rope as it wrapped itself around the drum in order to prevent knotting, crossing and uneven lapping. These shears, or clippers, were formed of thick beams of wood and attached to either arm was a long wooden roller, against which the rope pressed, thus preventing friction and the consequent wearing away and fraying of the rope, although this occasionally did happen.

A station on the Blackwall Railway. The line, which opened in 1846 and ran from Fenchurch Street to Blackwall Pier, provided a direct rail link from the East India Docks into the City. In the foreground can be seen the wire rope that pulled the carriages. The Blackwall Railway closed in 1926 soon after the General Strike and the tracks lay derelict for many years until the Docklands Light Railway opened, using the same viaducts from Fenchurch Street to Poplar. It was later extended and there is now a Blackwall and an East India Dock station a short distance from the original station.

CHAPTER THREE
SILKWEAVERS

Mrs Mary Waite at her spinning wheel, Cranbrook Street, Bethnal Green, April 1930. She was paid a visit by Mrs Baldwin, who watched a demonstration of silkweaving. Mary Waite was one of the last surviving silkweavers of Huguenot descent in the Bethnal Green area.

When the Edict of Nantes (1595) was revoked by the French government in 1685, the French Protestants or Huguenots, started to leave the country in large numbers to escape persecution. They sought refuge in Holland, Switzerland, Prussia and England. In the first year of the persecutions some 15,000 Huguenots arrived in London alone. Among those who came to England were silkweavers from Lyons and Tours and they settled in Spitalfields, traditionally an area which attracted immigrants. Here rents were low and the area had a strong and established weaving tradition. They brought many of their secrets with them, and for a time silkweaving flourished, helped by a law prohibiting the importation of French silk.

But silkweaving was not the only trade the Huguenots brought with them. They were also silversmiths and jewellers, clock and watchmakers, and mathematical and surgical-instrument makers.

It was estimated that there were 20,000 looms being worked in the Spitalfields area by the mid-eighteenth century. However, with the introduction of mechanized looms and the importing of cheap calico, the industry suffered a decline. Bad practices among the journeymen also contributed to the sporadic unrest and violence in the community. Various Spitalfields Acts were passed in 1773, 1792 and 1801 regulating wages, also in 1773 a Prohibition Act was passed on foreign silks but the government only partially succeeded in averting economic and social disorder. In 1824 and 1826, however, the acts were repealed and duties were imposed on foreign silks. Despite this the foreign silks were still cheaper and continued to undercut the local industry, leading to widespread poverty in Spitalfields. A House of Commons committee set up in 1831 to investigate the position found that the number of workers in the area entirely dependent on the industry was 50,000, and an equal number were indirectly dependent.

Before the end of the eighteenth century two main groups of weavers existed. They were firstly the master weavers who made only the finest grade material, and secondly piece-working cottage workers who were given out work by the master weavers for popular brocades and damasks. As trade declined, middlemen, instead of master craftsmen who were proud of the work of their employees, began to appear. These middlemen knew nothing about the craft and were interested only in obtaining the materials at low prices for the warehouses. Many of the ordinary workers were put out of work, only the finest craftsmen being able to continue their trade.

Finally, in 1860 the duty on French silks was abolished, the weavers of Spitalfields could no longer compete with cheap imports and they left their looms to seek other employment, in the docks and in other trades. This decline of course caused great distress among the weaving community. A few moved to the north of England, but many became poverty stricken and only a few survived into the 1930s. Now the only working silk looms can be found at Braintree in Essex. Warner and Sons, who went to Braintree in 1895 with six families of Bethnal Green silkweavers, is the best-known survivor today. Sir Frank Warner, who wrote a book on silkweaving in 1914, said that forty-six workshops were still occupied by weavers in Cranbrook Street and Alma Road, now Doric Road, to the east of Bethnal Green, some distance away from the old centre at Spitalfields. At that time there were 114 workers employed in weaving. By 1931 the number had dropped to a mere eleven and the last loom stopped at the beginning of the Second World War. These last weavers used to produce handkerchiefs, tie and umbrella silks, scarves and wraps of high quality. The most famous of the last weavers was George Doree, who wove the cloth for the coronation robe of Edward VII. The coronation robes of George V and Queen Elizabeth II were made by Warner and Sons of Braintree.

The Huguenots left behind an enduring legacy of their presence in the surviving buildings in roads such as Fournier Street, Wilkes Street and Princelet Street. The rows of early eighteenth-century weavers' houses built in the area are the oldest houses of the industry remaining today. A small colony of weavers' houses existed at the extreme eastern corner of Bethnal Green, in the area of Cranbrook Street and Doric Road. The sound of a loom in operation is very loud, and in order to reduce noise, many of these cottages had waste cloth or sawdust packed between the floor of the workshop and the ceiling below.

Quite a number of houses built in the early nineteenth century had two or even three floors above the ground floor devoted to weaving, the greater part of the house being used as a workshop. Life must have been very hard for the weavers at this time, the average working day lasting between twelve and fourteeen hours. Many of the weavers suffered from chest complaints which they attributed to spending so much time leaning against the bar of the loom. The workrooms were seldom aired, the windows being purposely sealed to keep the humidity of the air in the room high. This prevented the very fine silk threads from snapping, but what was probably more important for the weavers of the time, it made the cloth heavier so that it appeared to be of greater value.

It was in this area that the last of the silkweavers worked up to the beginning of the Second World War and it was here that George Doree, the most skilled of the last silkweavers lived. These houses have all been cleared and the area is now Cranbrook Estate.

Weavers race from Type Street, Bethnal Green, early twentieth century.

Mr Charles Waite at his loom at 45 Cranbrook Street, Bethnal Green, *c.* 1935. Charles and Mary Waite were among the last silkweavers living in this area.

Weavers' cottages, 6–10 Crossland Square, Bethnal Green, 1954. At the time this picture was taken, these cottages were about to be demolished under a slum-clearance scheme. They are, however, fine examples of weavers' dwellings with the upper floor having large windows intended to provide as much daylight as possible for silkweavers.

A Spitalfields weaver at work, June 1895. While the husband is using the loom, on the right the wife sits with the remains of their meal. Note the large windows to the rear, which let in as much light as possible.

A silkweaving loom at 42 Alma Road, Spitalfields, 1909. By the end of the nineteenth century the silkweaving trade in Spitalfields had declined from what had been a thriving industry in the eighteenth century. Two women can be seen hard at work at their looms.

Thomas and Horace Hilliard, at 13 St Andrews Street, Bethnal Green, 1927. The two elderly brothers were silkweavers for many years, and probably two of the last to ply their trade in the East End.

A Spitalfields loom and spinning wheel. The owner of the loom was Mr Payne, who brought it from Nuneaton, where he and his wife and parents had been ribbonweavers. The loom, known as a 'narrow loom', was used for making fringes and trimmings.

A Spitalfields loom with Jacquard attachment, late 1960s. This picture was taken by Halifax Photos Ltd (photographer Halifax Jacobs). What is perhaps surprising is the crudeness of the structure, with the rollers being weighed down by a dozen bricks!

CHAPTER FOUR

FACTORIES & FACTORY WORKERS

Allen & Hanbury's factory in Bethnal Green, 1913. The factory was destroyed by enemy bombs on 19 May 1918, and was rebuilt in 1922. Allen & Hanbury manufactured surgical instruments, as well as pharmaceuticals, drugs and medical supplies.

By the nineteenth century the East End of London had become a highly industrialized area. The canals provided a constant supply of water, and manufacturers were quick to take advantage of this. Some of the major manufacturing concerns were papermaking, ropemaking, sugar manufacturing, tobacco processing, soapmaking and matchmaking.

Paper mills were established in the early 1800s along the River Lea in East London. The paper produced was of poor quality, being heavily mixed with rags and other non-binding material. In the 1840s Mr Petrushkin opened a paper factory in the Bow Road. His paper was of better quality, as he used hemp. Although normally imported and expensive, the hemp Petrushkin used was from old ship's ropes, and ships in London's docks provided a steady supply, hence the expression 'money for old rope!' In 1860, Edward Lloyd opened a paper mill in Bow, initially using straw as a binding agent, then esparto grass from North Africa. His high-quality paper was soon in demand and Lloyd's Paper Mill at one time had 200 employees, working in 2 shifts of 12 hours, and earning between 10s and 13s a week. There were no set lunch hours, and workmen's wives or children usually brought their lunches to them on plates tied up in large red handkerchiefs. Another mill that used esparto grass was the firm Wiggins, Teape and Company, in Bromley by Bow. This firm is still in existence. However, with the disappearance of sailing ships, hemp became more difficult to acquire, and esparto was found to be too time consuming to process. To keep these and other mills supplied with materials, rag factories were established in Bow, the Isle of Dogs and Ratcliff. Washed, sorted and shredded rags provided the poorer quality paper needed for cheap literature and the growing demands of the newspaper world. The work of sorting rags was hard, dirty and very poorly paid, but hundreds of women were involved in this. Firms such as John Hill and Company of Millwall set up factories to repulp used or waste paper. Throughout the nineteenth and early twentieth centuries East London continued to produce good- and poor-quality paper and paper products, according to customers' needs. Most of the mills have now gone, including the Limehouse Paperboard Mills in Narrow Street, Limehouse, which closed in December 1987.

James John Frost established a ropemaking business in 1790 which grew to become one of the largest ropemakers in the country. Frost Brothers was one of several large established ropemakers in the East End of London, along with West and Co., Soanes and Co., at Bow, Huddart & Co. in Limehouse and Hawkins and Tipson's on the Isle of Dogs. Rope was manufactured mainly from manila and hemp, and was an essential commodity in the docks. The disappearance of sailing ships and the decline of the docks and the use of nylon in the production of rope and twine eventually saw the end of this major industry.

Tobacco was imported into the country, packed in large hogsheads and stored at the Tobacco Bonded Warehouses in Pennington Street, Ratcliffe Highway, which is now known as Tobacco Docks. The mass of tobacco stored here was so great that at any one time there would be more than 20,000 hogsheads, each containing 1,200 lb of tobacco. The tobacco was kept in bond until the duty was paid on it, when it would be sold to the manufacturer to be turned into cigars, tobacco for pipes or cigarettes and snuff.

There were several sugar manufacturers in the Stepney area, such as Martineau and Fairrie. Many of the early sugar bakers were of German origin and had set up their refineries in the City of London. Eventually they were driven out as the process of refining sugar involved the use of bone meal and animal blood, which produced a noxious odour, unbearable during the hot summer months.

Another major industry was brushmaking, which was both a factory and a home industry. G.B. Kent and Sons Ltd, manufacturers of brushes since the eighteenth century and one of the oldest established companies in Britain, originally had their head offices and factory at 11 Great Marlborough Street. However, when these premises became too small for the rapidly growing business, more buildings and land were acquired at 14–20 Robinson Road and 59 Approach Road, Victoria Park in Bethnal Green, where all the toothbrush manufacture was transferred to. According to the annual report of 1959, the company manufactured many different kinds of brushes: toilet, paint, household and industrial of the very best workmanship, which were exported all over the world. They were most renowned for their finest quality toilet brushes for hair, teeth, nails and shaving. At midsummer 1882 the work force numbered over 600, and 160 of these were employed making toothbrushes alone, 60 gross of which were turned out per week. The handles were made chiefly of bone which came direct from the London bone boilers. Only the leg bones of bullocks were used for good quality toothbrushes and the consumption of bones for this output of 60 gross required the produce of no less than 600 head of cattle weekly!

Bethnal Green Starch Works, 7 Old Ford Road, Bethnal Green, c. 1910. The Bethnal Green Starch Company, which was at the end of Old Ford Road, near the junction with Cambridge Heath Road, was acquired in the 1860s by J. & J. Colman of Norwich, better known for their tins of mustard. Colman's starch was manufactured here from July 1873. The factory closed in 1916, by which time it had taken over Nos 5–13. In 1923 Bethnal Green Council purchased the starch works for £10,000, demolished it and built York Hall Baths on the site.

Cigarette making at J. & S. Hill, cigar and cigarette manufacturers in Shoreditch. Women are seen making cigarettes by hand. Daisy Parsons, who was an East End Suffragette, recalled that as a young girl (in about 1910) she worked in a cigarette factory in Whitechapel, where she earned 2*d* for making a thousand cigarettes. Other cigar and cigarette manufacturers in East London were Godfrey Phillips, founded in 1844, at 112 Commercial Street. The firm employed about 3,000 workers, of whom 66–70 per cent were women, of which only 40 per cent belonged to a union.

Cigarette making at J. & S. Hill. The process of cigar making was pretty nearly the same wherever it was carried on. The cigar makers were seated in rows at their workbenches, each having their own clearly defined area to work in. A leaf of tobacco was spread out on the bench, and the cigar maker made gashes in the leaf, somewhat resembling the gores or stripes of a balloon. He then took up a few fragments of tobacco leaf, and rolled them up into a form nearly resembling that of a cigar. He next placed this cigar against a gauge or guide, formed from a piece of iron, and cut it to a given length. Finally, he laid a narrow strip of leaf on the bench, and rolled the cigar spirally in it, twisting one end to prevent the leaf from becoming loosened. All this was done with great rapidity, only a few seconds needed to complete one cigar. When the cigars were made, they were dried in different ways, according to the time when they were wanted for sale. Sometimes fresh roses were brought in and the petals were strewn on the tobacco leaf before rolling up. These were speciality cigars, and were very much in demand.

The Improved Omnibus patented and built by Adams and Co. at their Fairfield Road works, Bow, 1847. The carriage could convey thirteen passengers inside and fourteen passengers on the outside. They were charged 2*d* and 1*d* respectively. Adams and Co. went on to manufacture railway carriages at their works, before the land was acquired by Bryant and May for their match factory.

Worland's Wharf with barges on the foreshore at Bow Creek, 1927. The wharf stored tyres, which can be seen here being loaded into barges. The wharf was in Wharf Street, Canning Town, between Lea Shipbuilding Yard and Crown Wharf. On the opposite side of the river stood Creek Wharf and Poplar Gas Works. In common with many other East End factories and wharves, fire was an ever-present danger, and in 1935 the wharf was destroyed by a devastating blaze.

Women working in the Russian and Italian hemp preparing room. Rope was manufactured from a variety of fibres, but mainly manila hemp, sisal hemp, common hemp and coir, which was obtained from the husks of coconuts.

Binder-twine and trawl-twine spinning. The prepared Russian and Italian hemp is seen being fed into the spinning machines. The women operatives stood at their posts all the time they worked; feeding the fibre into the machines was particularly hard on their hands. As the average working week at Frost's lasted 54 hours, this meant they worked for 9 hours a day, 6 days a week.

The first process in spinning manila. The women are seen feeding the hemp up to the spreading machines, taken from the bales as they come from the Philippine Islands. The three machines seen here would have been capable of processing 120 bales of hemp per day.

Hand dressing manila fibre in the ropemaking factory of Frost Brothers, Commercial Road, 1906. The output at the factory was in the region of 100 tons of yarn and 120 tons of rope per week.

Messrs J. Evershed and Co., printers, Fairfield Road and 744 Old Ford Road, Bow, 1947. These are huge rolls of paper and reams on pallets, with a man operating a fork-lift truck ready to transport them.

J. Evershed and Co., 1947. The printing presses are seen at work.

Thames Plate Glass Co., Bow Creek, Poplar. The glassmaking firm stood on the ground that was later occupied by Messrs Baldwins (who retained some of the Glass House walls), as well as the Bow Creek Union Oil Mills, Fowler Sugar Refinery, The Thames Sack and Bag Factory, the LCC School and also the roadway which led to the above premises. At present the Pura Foods Factory occupies most of this area.

Until about 1875 the Glass House prospered, employing about 75 per cent of the inhabitants of Orchard House, Bow Creek, who were nearly all related. Plate glass was made there and sent all over the country, including all the glass used in the making of the Crystal Palace. However, by about 1875 the competition from the United States glass industry ruined the Orchard House factory and it closed down. A large proportion of the workers, both men and women, emigrated to New Albany, Indiana, USA, to pursue the same work. There were still a large number of descendants of the glass workers living in Orchard House up to the 1930s, the most numerous being the Lammins, the Scanlons and the Jeffries.

Workers line up alongside the lorries piled high with sacks of horsehair at the Stratford Hair Company, Sugar House Lane, Stratford. William Stanway, manager, is standing on the far right in overalls. Horsehair was used to stuff mattresses, as well as being woven into coarse blankets.

Workers at Edward Cook & Co. London, soap manufacturers, Bow, 1915. The firm was established by Edward Cook in Norwich in the eighteenth century. Edward Cook died in 1831, and the firm moved shortly afterwards to Goodman's Yard, Whitechapel. In 1859 a factory was opened at Bow, on the banks of the River Lea, near the site of what was known as King John's Palace. The company grew to be one of the largest manufacturers of soap and related products. The men seen here are working at a soap mill, processing toilet soap. Ribbons of pure soap fall from the mill to the carrier, untouched by hand. The soft soap would then be poured into moulds and stamped.

Women working in the wrapping department of Cook's London in their factory in Bow, known as 'The Soapery', 1915. Here the finished soap was individually wrapped and boxed. The most popular brand was Throne Toilet Soap, whose bouquet was likened to the fragrance of a Devonshire cottage garden on a lovely May morning! Edward Cook and Co.'s soap and perfume factory at The Soapery in Cook's Road, Bow remained in business until the end of the Second World War. The company was then taken over by John Knight Ltd, another well-known soap manufacturer with premises in Wapping.

Allen & Hanbury's factory in Bethnal Green, 1927. Men working in the Machine Room and Printing Department. Besides pharmaceuticals and related items, Allen & Hanbury also printed all their own labels, leaflets, pamphlets, medical literature and books, catalogues and even calendars.

Workers in the packed drugs department at Allen & Hanbury's factory in Bethnal Green, 1927. Tablets and dry goods are packed according to chemists' and druggists' orders prior to despatch.

Wall Paper Manufacturers Ltd, 1949. John Allan founded his wallpaper business by commencing block printing in a room in Hackney Road in 1812. In about 1846, he and his sons, John Charles and George William, moved into new premises, covering about 10 acres on the banks of the River Lea, and here with the aid of two new machines they built up a flourishing business. In 1874 the firm moved into a new and specially built factory in Wick Lane. Some eighteen years after John Allan the founder died the business, with its 200 employees, was sold to John and James Cockshut. In 1899 the business became part of the newly formed company the Wall Paper Manufacturers, of which John Cockshut was appointed chairman in its second year. The Allan Cockshut branch had an extensive export trade, making special wallpapers for the Indian and Chinese markets and had a large share of the South American trade.

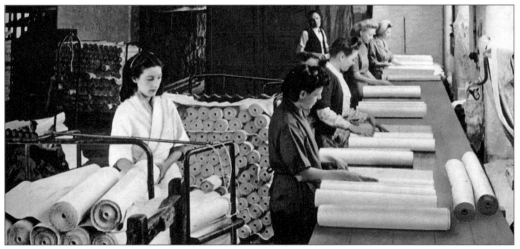

Rolls of wallpaper being packed for despatch at Wall Paper Manufacturers Ltd, 1949. The factory survived the Second World War and appeared to be flourishing, but on 6 May 1966, 18 months after it was taken over by Reed Paper Group, it was announced that the factory, which then employed 350 people, was to shut because of shortage of labour in the East End of London, and by September the factory was completely closed.

Naphtha Distillery, Copperfield Road, Bow, *c.* 1903. The company of Jones & Mason, Methylated Spirit makers, is first listed in trade directories at 1a Butcher Row, Ratcliff, and moved to Copperfield Road in 1882. Jones and Company (Methylators) Ltd is finally listed in the trade directories in 1949. The 1881 census records Henry Jones, aged forty-two, as living at 41 St Pauls Road, Mile End Old Town, which was in the vicinity of Copperfield Road. With him were his wife Jemima, son Henry J., twenty-two, and daughter Amelia, eleven, born in Mile Old Town, which would place the family in the neighbourhood from 1870.

The interior of the sugar refinery of Messrs Fairrie, Brothers and Co., situated behind Whitechapel Church. The refinery consisted mainly of two ranges of buildings. The hogsheads of sugar, each weighing from 4 to 18 cwt, were brought in waggons from the West India Docks. Here a worker is seen breaking open a hogshead which contained the dark moist brown sugar. During the refining process, raw sugar was mixed with lime water and bullock's blood and the accumulated scum containing impurities was drawn off. The liquid sugar was then passed through fine mesh strainers until a clear brown liquid resulted. This was refined through charcoal, made from burnt animal bone, which removed the colour from the liquid. Finally, the clear liquid sugar was put through a process of evaporation in a vacuum until it began to crystallize, and was then formed into loaf sugar in moulds. When the loaves had been left drying for several hours, they were wrapped in paper and placed in an oven or stoving room until thoroughly dried. Working under these conditions was very hot and often dangerous, and the men generally worked stripped to the waist.

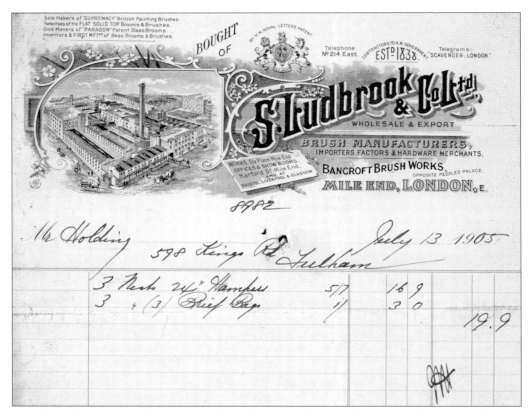

Letterhead of brush manufacturers S. Ludbrook & Co. Ltd, 1905. Their Bancroft Brush Works were situated at Ely Place, Mile End, opposite the People's Palace, while their offices and showrooms were at Harford Street. The factory was established in 1838 and produced all kinds of brooms and brushes.

Arthur Dellow and Co., basketmakers and brush manufacturers, were at 633 Commercial Road until 1910. The Dellows were traditional basketweavers from the Shadwell area from as early as 1825, and Joseph, Annie, Frederick and Arthur Dellow were all basketmakers.

CHAPTER FIVE

MATCHMAKERS

Women working by the conveyor belt at the Bryant and May Match Factory in Fairfield Road Bow, c. 1920. The machine on the right of the picture is seen making the outer cases of the matchboxes, which are then pushed off automatically on to the conveyor which takes them to the drying chamber.

Up to the mid-nineteenth century, matchmaking in Britain was a cottage industry, based in private houses, back rooms and gloomy attics. Many of the children employed in the industry showed signs of phossy jaw, or phosphorus necrosis. The disease, which attacked the jawbone, causing it to crumble away, was attributed to the handling of white phosphorus, and its absorption via the mouth and gums. The greatest concentration of match factories was to be found in the East End of London. The Bryant and May Factory, Fairfield Works, was perhaps the largest of these, together with Bell's in Bromley by Bow.

In 1843 William Bryant and Francis May formed a partnership, and the firm Bryant and May, provision merchants, was founded. They both belonged to the Society of Friends, or Quakers. In 1850, a meeting with Carl Lundstrom, a Swedish matchmaker, was to change their fortunes forever – he sold them two boxes (cases) of matches. Bryant and May became the sole distributors of Lundstrom's matches, and when Johan Lundstrom went on to invent the first safety match, patented in 1855, he sold the British patent rights to Bryant and May. However, the demand for matches from the British public was so great that Bryant and May decided to set up their own factory for the manufacture of safety matches, with the help of Johan Lundstrom.

In 1860, Bryant and May found an ideal site in Fairfield Road. A 3-acre site containing a disused crinoline factory, a candlemaking company and a rope works was bought and Johan Lundstrom designed the factory and advised on machine installation. Throughout the years that the Bryant and May Match Factory operated from the Fairfield Works, the buildings were continually being enlarged and remodelled. In 1866 Francis May retired from business and the firm was run entirely by William Bryant and his sons. Wilberforce Bryant became the new head of the firm, and the other sons, Theodore, Arthur and Frederick, were directors.

In 1871 the government proposed a match tax – $\frac{1}{2}d$ on all matchboxes. People feared that this would lead to a closure of many small factories and loss of employment. Queen Victoria herself expressed the view that the tax would cause severe hardship for the women and children of the East End. A great demonstration was held in Victoria Park and the crowd, led by women and children from Bow, carrying banners and flags, marched to Westminster. The majority of demonstrators were from the Bryant and May Factory. Arriving at Parliament, the marchers were stopped by a huge police force. The resulting bloody battle and violent methods employed by the police to restrain the crowd proved to be a turning point. The proposal for the tax was withdrawn. To commemorate this event a public subscription was set up by Bryant and May, and a drinking fountain was built in the Bow Road from the proceeds. It was unveiled on 5 October 1872. This is the monument that the matchgirls referred to as having been paid for 'with their blood', for they were all docked a shilling from their wages to pay for it. The fountain was demolished in 1953, during the widening of the Bow Road.

In 1884 Bryant and May decided to convert into a public limited company, and 60,000 shares of £5 were quickly snapped up. Shares were also allotted to heads of departments and long-serving employees. But there were soon new challenges to face.

In 1888, the Fabian Society heard a lecture from Clementina Black on the conditions of matchworkers in the East End of London. She stated that in factories such as Bryant and May the continual exposure to phosphorus, and lack of health checks for the workers, led to a high incidence of illness and phossy jaw. Some manufacturers on the continent had switched to the safer phosphorus, but the Fairfield Works was reluctant to do so as it would affect the profits, which that year were a record 20 per cent.

Annie Besant, a journalist and a member of the Fabian Society, was in the audience and she decided to investigate the matter, together with Leigh Hunt and W.T. Stead. After speaking to some of the workers at the factory, she published an article in the *Link* – entitled 'White Slavery in London'. On 5 July two girls who had spoken to her were sacked. Annie Besant returned to the factory, and distributed leaflets urging the workers to come out on strike. Some 1,200 girls and women struck work. The events that followed were to have far-reaching effects, not only for the matchmakers, but for workers everywhere. The strikers were supported by William Morris and George Bernard Shaw, among other celebrities, and held marches and demonstrations in Victoria Park, Mile End and Hyde Park. On 21 July the strike was called off following a meeting with Bryant and May and the London Trades Council. Annie Besant went on to form the Union of Women Matchmakers.

While many of the more scandalous charges made against the factory owners were subsequently disproved, some of the concessions they agreed to, such as abolishing fines for breaches of conduct, stopping the deductions for paste and brushes made on boxmakers and insisting on a separate dining room for women workers, show that some of the charges were true. Bryant and May continued to use homeworkers for the manufacture of boxes when demand was high. These workers were paid a pittance for their work and had to collect the material for the boxes from the factory. They provided their own paste to glue the parts together, as well as string, which held the drying boxes, and had to return the finished boxes to the factory.

However, the continued use of the yellow or white phosphorus remained a danger to workers for the following ten years, until the discovery in 1898 of the non-poisonous sesquisulphide of phosphorus. In 1900 Bryant and May purchased the British patent rights to it, and in 1908 they offered the licence free to all United Kingdom matchmakers on the condition that the government banned the use of yellow phosphorus.

The present Fairfield Works building was erected in 1911. It was modelled on the Diamond Works in Liverpool. During the time of the Matchgirls' Strike the factory was the large building that was entered from the Wick Lane gate. It is part of the present building complex still in existence today, which is now called the Bow Quarter and contains luxury apartments. The Fairfield Works were enlarged and rebuilt during the 1950s and 1960s. In 1971 the manufacture of woodstick matches ceased, and in 1979/80 the match works closed and the head office was transferred to High Wycombe.

George Lansbury MP for Bow and Poplar and a matchmaker's child, 1912. The young lad carrying the bundle on his head has just collected the material for making matchboxes from the match factory. The whole family would spend hours making up the matchboxes, which would then be returned to the factory. Lansbury lost his seat in 1912, following a by-election after declaring himself in favour of women's suffrage.

A mother and four children are engaged in making matchboxes at home. Matchboxmaking was carried out in homes by women outworkers, who collected the required materials from the match factory and then returned the finished boxes to the factory and were paid as little as 6d per gross. The returns on this form of homework were extremely poor.

The Bryant and May Match Factory, 1961. Matchsticks having been dipped and dried are now moving towards the boxes to be filled, while a woman worker keeps an eye on the conveyor belt carrying the inner boxes.

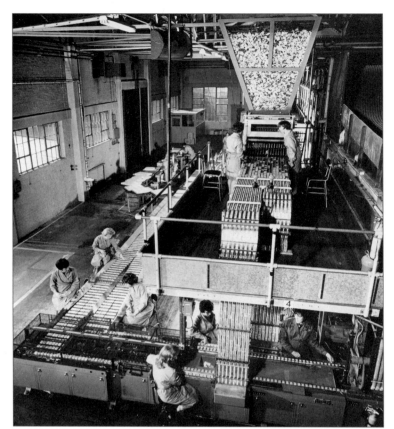

The Bryant and May Match Factory, 1960s. The output side of a matchmaking machine. The dried matches (extreme bottom right) are moving down towards the inner boxes (bottom right). The outer boxes are moving down to the inner boxes which are slid into them (bottom centre). The closed boxes then pass along the inspection conveyor (left) to the wrapping machine (left background). The women are seated at the conveyor belt, a great improvement on the earlier picture of the factory, which showed that women had to stand all day at their machines.

Women working in the printing department of the Bryant and May Match Factory, c. 1920. All labels for Bryant and May matchboxes, including Brymay Safety, Swan and Puck, were printed at the factory. The outer wrappers for dozen and gross packets were also printed on the premises. The average annual production at the time was in the region of 2,000 million labels, or about 40 million labels a week.

CHAPTER SIX

METALWORKERS & FOUNDRIES

Strips of metal are being passed through the machines to be cut at the cutting room at the Royal Mint.

The construction of the buildings housing the Royal Mint was begun by James Johnson, the Surveyor to the Royal Mint, and completed in 1818 by Robert Smirke, after the death of Johnson. The site of the Royal Mint was once occupied by the Cistercian Abbey of St Mary of Grace, founded in 1349 by Edward III. Following the dissolution of the abbey, Henry VIII granted title of the land to Sir Arthur Darcey, who pulled down the buildings and built a victualling depot for the Royal Navy. This later became a government storehouse for tobacco, which was subsequently demolished for the building of the Mint.

In the old days the metal for coins was cut with shears, and afterwards shaped and stamped by the hammer, and the edges were not milled, the result being that few pieces were either exactly round or contained the exact quantity of metal. The pictures on the following pages, from 1938, show the procedure for converting metal into coin. First the metal is melted into bars of the composition prescribed by law and of sizes suitable for the particular coins that are to be made. Then it is rolled under pressure to the requisite thickness of several tons of such bars received from the Melting House. This is followed by the cutting of coinage blanks of the requisite diameter and weight, and then the annealing of the blanks in gas-heated furnaces and the removal of the oxide – formed in this process – by blanching in dilute acid. Once this is finished the blanks are impressed with the milling and the two faces with the authorized designs in presses each capable of producing 200 coins a minute. Finally the coins are counted by automatic machines to make up bags of predetermined values.

The Whitechapel Bell Foundry, Mears and Stainbank, situated in the Whitechapel Road, is one of the very few traditional industries to survive to the present day. The foundry originated in Elizabethan times when Robert Mot began making bells, some of which are still in existence. All the eight bells at Westminster Abbey came from Whitechapel, between 1583 and 1919. The bells of St Paul's Cathedral, the famous 'Bow Bells', 'Great Tom' of Lincoln, and 'Big Ben' at Westminster are just some of the great bells to have been cast here. Many hundreds of bells have been exported to Canada and the USA, the most famous being the 'Liberty Bell'. Bellfounding techniques have changed very little over the hundreds of years, and the process is both intricate and laborious. The core or mould that forms the inside shape of the bell is built up of loam and specially made curved bricks, while the cope, or outer mould, for the bell is formed with loam inside a cast-iron moulding case. After being dried in an oven, the moulds are given a coating of graphite before being clamped together. The molten bell metal is then poured into the mould, which after being allowed to cool, is broken open to reveal the bell.

The gold melting house at the Royal Mint.

Pouring molten gold into moulds at the Royal Mint, 1898.

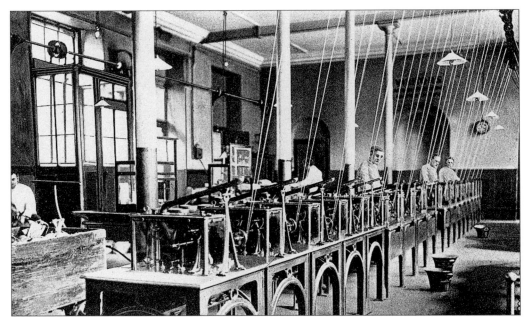

The weighing room at the Royal Mint, where coins are weighed and counted before being bagged for despatch.

The silver smelting room, the Royal Mint, 1898.

The bells of Shoreditch at the foundry of Messrs John Warner & Sons Ltd (Bell Founders), Spelman Street, Spitalfields, *c.* 1930. The foundry was established in 1763.

Recasting the 'Great Bell' (Big Ben) for the clock tower at the new Houses of Parliament, 1858. The recasting of the 'Great Bell' took place at the bell foundry of Messrs Mears and Stainbank, Whitechapel Road. The process of breaking up the old bell began on 17 February and lasted nearly a week. The pattern of the new bell began in November of the previous year, and the designer was a Mr Denison. The making of the mould commenced on 18 December and was continued without interruption until it was finally put together and rammed up. 'Big Ben' was the largest bell made at the Whitechapel Bell Foundry, and weighed an impressive 13½ tons. The process of casting is an intricate and labourious one. The mould consists first of the core, which is built up of bricks, covered with clay and formed to the shape of the inside of the bell by means of a board, called the sweep or crook. The pit to contain the mould for Big Ben was 13 ft deep; the extreme height of the bell was 7½ ft.

The factory interior at the United Horseshoe and Nail Company in Wharf Road, Cubitt Town, on the Isle of Dogs, 1907. The company, which employed 150 men, went into liquidation in 1909, following a decline in orders. In 1907 the company suffered a severe blow when they lost a government contract for 100,000 pairs of horseshoes, which went instead to an American firm. The advent of the motor car heralded the demise of an industry which had existed since man had first learned to harness horses. In this factory alone, some 1,800 tons of horseshoes were made annually. They were manufactured out of scrap iron, which was thrown into a furnace. Red-hot molten iron was then removed from it and machine hammered into iron bars. These were reheated and fed through rollers which created long and thin flat rods easily cut into various lengths. Horseshoes were made by heating and twisting the flat rods, after which nail holes were drilled into them.

Commercial Gas Company Munitions Foundry, *c.* 1915. On the extreme right is Miss W.N. Anderson, junior typist and messenger, and Mr C.G. Madgett, chief clerk. Unfortunately, we do not know the names of the other workers. In the foreground are the wooden moulds for casting gun barrels.

Women workers at the Commercial Gas Company Munitions Foundry, *c.* 1915. They are standing by a saw being used to cut up logs which were used as the outer case for the casting process.

Two men with a barrel of molten metal at the Commercial Gas Company Munitions Foundry, *c.* 1915. Note that the man in the distance has two handles to hold which he uses to turn the barrel. The man nearest the camera has only one handle to hold.

Metal being poured into cases at the Commercial Gas Company Munitions Foundry, *c.* 1915. Inside the wooden cases is a half of the gun case. Soot and sand is used to settle the molten metal so that a gun case can be formed.

Workers at the Commercial Gas Company Munitions Foundry, *c.* 1915. These men are making the moulds, pouring molten metal into the moulds and shaking out the metal cases.

Buck and Hickman Ltd, Engineers and Toolmakers, 30 Whitechapel Road, *c.* 1930. The firm of Buck and Hickman was founded in Whitechapel by John Hickman in about 1828 as small iron and steel merchants. They became a limited company at the turn of the century, and then expanded rapidly, opening branches in Birmingham, Manchester and Glasgow.

Workmen at Buck and Hickman's iron and steel store, 30 Whitechapel Road, *c.* 1930. The 1960 directory placed the machine-tool company at 2–22 Whitechapel Road, on the corner of Adler Street.

CHAPTER SEVEN

THE RAG TRADE

A tailor's workshop in East London, early twentieth century.

The centres of London's clothing market in the seventeenth and eighteenth centuries were the Houndsditch Rag Fair and the Rosemary Lane Rag Fair, which took place in the shadow of the Tower of London. Here dealers and tailors looked through the material, while ordinary people examined the second-hand clothing, and the poor picked over the rags. This way of life remained unchanged for 200 years.

Most of the cloth available in England was imported from the continent, a small amount of inferior cloth being made on hand looms in this country. Superior fabrics were fashioned into clothing for the aristocracy by the few master tailors who had migrated from the continent, and those who had learnt the trade from them. The middle classes bought fabric that was sewn into garments by skilled needlewomen. For them it was not important that their clothing fitted, so long as the material was durable and the garment presentable. The working classes wore rough garments made from cast-off clothing or of inferior material and their smocks and gowns fitted where they touched, the only criteria being decency and warmth.

During this time the Jewish connection with the garment trade became established among the second-hand clothes and rag dealers of the Houndsditch antique mart. It was mainly the German and the Dutch Jews who formed the bulk of the traders, and by 1850 the much-hatted 'Old Clo' man was a familiar figure as he trundled from his lodgings in Rosemary Lane to sell his tattered wares to such merchants as Isaacs or Simmonds & Levy at the rag fair near the Tower of London. These characters wore several hats: they were for sale. The better garments were 'clobbered' (renovated) and then sold by them to the poor.

Spitalfields was the main centre for tailoring, with a few shops in Wapping, Whitechapel and Ratcliff. Clothing and yarn was dyed and bleached in what was locally called the Tenterfields area and laid out in the open to dry. Soon, more workshops began to open in Whitechapel, Houndsditch and the Minories, turning out clothing for a growing market. The system of using outworkers became more common, with people working in their own homes on individual items supplied to them by master tailors and middlemen. This form of employment grew into appalling drudgery, with women and children working far into the night to complete the work and earn a few pennies. The sweating system was beginning to take shape. More and more factories opened in the East End of London, although they did not have machinery, but were places where employees worked together in a controlled environment.

By the mid-nineteenth century working conditions had become dire. Improvements in the production of coal and steel paved the way for mechanization, which together with increasing supplies of cotton from America made fabrics more easily and cheaply available. New methods of production led to increased output, and more people found employment though not necessarily better wages.

In the 1850s two inventions, Isaac Singer's treadle-operated sewing machine and John Barran's bandsaw which was able to cut through many thicknesses of material at one time, revolutionized the tailoring industry. In particular, they had a profound effect on the clothing industry in East London which had for centuries relied on the basic tools of the trade: scissors, a tape measure and needle and cotton. For a century these two new machines dominated the machine shops and factories, and their electric-powered successors are still very much in use. By the 1860s four-fifths of male tailors were based in their own homes and either obtained work there through a sweater, or collected it from a warehouse two or three times a week. Most of their work was slop work or government work, which meant that, even when there was plenty to be had, tailors could only expect to earn about 13s a week, hardly enough to maintain the family, and invariably wives and children helped out too. Whole families worked in poor light, with the material lying on unswept floors or used to cover up sick members of the family or to give extra warmth on the bed. Frequently it was lice-infested and the contractor often had his garments returned to him in a less than satisfactory condition. Some tailors bought or hired their own sewing machines and managed to increase their earnings, but the growing availability of machines only served to lower the prices paid for piece work.

Conditions among the East London dressmakers and needlewomen were no better. Although much of this work was done in the West End and the City, there were a number of workshops in Houndsditch and Whitechapel. In 1861 the London clothing industry employed about 5,000 men and 24,000 women. Most of the girls worked from between twelve and seventeen hours a day, they lived out and were paid between 6 and 9s a week plus tea. It was impossible to support oneself on these wages alone, and many struggled to improve their skills in the hope of increasing their earnings. Dressmakers and seamstresses working long hours into the night aged far more quickly than girls in service, and they were often old at forty, their eyes strained, their brows furrowed and their fingers bent and gnarled.

With the resulting massive increase in production at much lower cost and the creation of a wave of new jobs, the way was paved for hundreds of journeymen stitchers and the 100,000 Jewish immigrants fleeing the pogroms of Eastern Europe to make their mark in clothes manufacturing. Between 1880 and 1914, Jewish migrants arrived from Poland, Germany and Russia. The ultimate destination for many of these families was America, and some of them did indeed continue their journey onwards to this 'promised land'. Those Jews who settled in the East End, albeit for a short time, found work in the clothing industry, and master tailors were soon setting up sweating dens and employing 'greeners' or new arrivals on the lowest possible wages.

Tailors and clothing workers in search of employment took themselves to the 'pig market' in the Whitechapel Road. Here immigrants, both Jews and Irish would gather and master tailors would move among them shouting out for a machinist, a presser, or a tailoring hand. There were many applicants for each job available, and a great deal of haggling took place, the work going to the man who would accept the worst job at the lowest rate of pay. Bribery and corruption were commonplace and an accepted part of the process, which was brutal to the penniless immigrant.

The arrival of mechanization changed the whole concept of the tailoring industry. Where previously whole coats, shirts, dresses, gowns etc. were made under the domestic or workshop system, 'specialists' now concentrated on just buttonholes, lapels, sleeves, pockets, pleating, padding, or button-covering. When each job was complete the clothing was returned to the sweater for passing on to the next worker, or for finishing. The link between home and workshop or factory was maintained by the little men, still remembered by some today, who were to be seen shuffling along the Commercial Road and Whitechapel Road with large quantities of material or unfinished clothing on their backs in all weathers.

While working conditions in the backstreet workshops were appalling, the factories were only slightly better. They provided a little more space and light, but the floors were strewn with cotton and waste material, tables covered with work and boxes where workers kept their scissors, needles, cotton and so on. With so much rubbish around there were frequent accidents and there was always a risk of fire. There were no cupboards, and little care was taken of the work of other people – half-finished clothing was thrown on the floor and often trodden on. The noise from such machines as there were was frightening, and there were no safety guards. One reason for the continued success of the East London garment industry can be attributed to the government contracts for uniforms and overcoats which came largely to this area, chiefly because it was cheaper and was more likely to be completed within the deadlines.

However, as other industries began to apply better conditions, so they were introduced to the clothing industry and in the early 1900s the working day was 8 a.m. to 7 p.m. (dusk on Fridays), with no work on Saturdays, although Sundays were often full working days. A minimum wage of 1s per hour was established. These improvements were slow to take shape, but were becoming effective by the start of the First World War.

In the meantime, health authorities were bringing in legislation controlling public health and sanitation, and paid particular attention to the small workshops. As late as 1930 almost half of all those in the clothing industry in the East End worked for firms employing twenty-five people or less. With the increasing demand for space, many of these workshops and small factories moved to Bow, Stratford and West Ham.

Some trades have disappeared from the area. The cloth cap trade, which in 1921 employed 1,200 people, 900 of them women, has gone, and few people wear cloth caps these days. Crinolines and shawls, cloaks and waistcoats, cravats and spats have all disappeared too. In 1938 western Stepney was home to many ladies' tailors but by 1958 there was a considerable reduction in numbers, particularly near the City borders. In the Bethnal Green area, twenty-six firms in 1938 had dwindled to just ten in 1958. Just before the Second World War there were twenty-eight workshops in Albert Gardens but by 1958 there were nine. The little firms disappeared, swallowed up by the larger concerns and market forces. Clothing is now mass-produced on an international scale and large stores and specialist clothing shops import much of their clothing from overseas, where labour is cheap.

By the early 1950s many rag traders, great and small, had migrated once more, this time to the West End. Jewish outdoor workers in the East End have been replaced by members of the Bangladeshi community, who have taken over the bulk of the wholesale garment industry. The trend in the cash-and-carry clothing trade, with companies selling throughout the week and on Sundays, has become an established practice, although the Aldgate end of Commercial Road is still the heart of the rag trade, but the names that predominate are no longer Jewish but Asian.

Wolf Cohen's bespoke tailoring establishment at 256 Roman Road, *c.* 1904. The shop opened for business in April 1904.

Letterhead of Richard Evans & Company, dated 7 May 1887. The factory of the Mantle, Dress and Upholstery Trimming manufacturers was at Hollybush Gardens, Bethnal Green; it was the subject of an enquiry into slum conditions in the area. The company had their warehouse and showroom at 24–6 Watling Street.

The Indiarubber waterproof works, Old Farm House, Stepney, 1855. That year the factory, owned by George Spill, won a large government contract for the manufacture of waterproof clothing for the army in the Crimea. The order, for 50,000 waterproof suits and several thousand pairs of waterproof sheets, required within forty days, had the factory working day and night without ceasing, until the order was completed. Spill's Waterproof Factory was at King John's Palace, Stepney Green, in the vicinity of St Dunstan's church.

A room occupied by a military tailor and his family at 10 Hollybush Place, Bethnal Green, *Illustrated London News*, October 1863. Hollybush Place, a small turning off Bethnal Green Road, just behind Paradise Row, had gained notoriety during an inquest into the death of a child which determined that the cause of death was blood poisoning, due to the filth and squalor of the neighbourhood in which he lived. The depiction of the tailor and his assistants hard at work in a room with just one chair and an ironing board was an all too familiar sight in the East End. In this neighbourhood whole families occupied single rooms, and bandbox and luciferbox makers, caneworkers, clothespegmakers, shoemakers and tailors all toiled endlessly, earning only just enough to keep them from absolute starvation.

Women workers at Milns, Cartwright, Reynolds & Co. Ltd, government contractors, at Sugar Loaf Walk, Bethnal Green, *c.* 1915. This factory, which was situated in a lane behind Bethnal Green Museum, made army uniforms. Women, who were taken on to replace men sent to fight in the First World War, were expected to work a sixteen-hour day, seven days a week. On the extreme left is Elizabeth Coe, with her sister Ethel standing next to her in full view.

Sadak Schneiders and Son, wholesale clothiers, 35–7 Durward Street, Whitechapel, during the First World War. A family business handed down from father to son, it was founded in Spitalfields in 1843 by Sadak Schneiders who came to London from Holland in the early nineteenth century. The firm also made caps at an adjoining premises. The head office of S. Schneiders and Son and their London factory was in Durward Street, and Schneiders later opened large factories at Rochester and Portsmouth as well. The firm was one of the first in the clothing industry to introduce a five-day week, and by the 1950s could boast of large staff canteens, medical services, as well as a fortnight's holiday with pay for their workers. On the extreme left wearing a cap is Harry Botchin, next to him, making army blankets, is Mr Frankenstein, in the centre foreground is Harry Klein and the man posing on the right, with a moustache is Abraham Botchin.

J. Steiner's tailoring workshop on the
top floor of 5 Fordham Street, Stepney,
1933. Annie Steiner was listed as the
householder in 1933, in 1935 Ray
Steiner and in the following year,
Lazarus Steiner. However, 5 Fordham
Street did not appear to be a business
establishment.

Poster of the Jewish Tailors' Strike,
issued by the Tailors' Strike Committee,
from the White Hart, Greenfield Street,
Commercial Road, 16 September 1889.
The leader of the Jewish Tailors' Union
was Lewis Lyons. It is interesting to
note the demands of the strikers: the
working day to be from 8 a.m. to
8 p.m. with an interval of one hour for
dinner and half an hour for tea; meals
to be had off the premises; four hours
overtime only to be allowed per week;
no more than two hours overtime to be
worked in one day; and the first
two hours overtime to be paid at the
ordinary rate, and the second
two hours at the rate of time and a
half. The strikers met at the Princes
Street Dramatic Club and at the
Hanbury Club.

GREAT STRIKE OF LONDON TAILORS

FELLOW WORKERS,

A report has been circulated that the Tailors' Strike is over. While we emphatically deny this report, and declare that

THE STRIKE IS NOT OVER,

we wish to bring the facts of the real state of affairs before your notice.

On Thursday night, 12th inst., after arrangements had been made for a conference between the Committees of the Men and Masters, we, together with the Committee of the West London District of the Amalgamated Society of Tailors, met the Masters' Committee. After a whole night's sitting, the Conference on Friday Morning unanimously agreed upon the following conditions for the settlement of the strike—provided only the strikers accept them, namely—

That a document be drawn up, signed by the Head Officers of the Master Tailors' Association, of the Strike Committee, of the Machinists' and Pressers' Societies (Printed copies of this document to be countersigned by each employer and hung up in each workshop), declaring—

1. The working day to be from 8 a.m. to 8 p.m., with the interval of one hour for dinner and half-an-hour for tea.
2. The meals to be had off the premises.
3. Four hours overtime only to be allowed per week.
4. No more than two hours overtime to be worked in one day; and
5. The first two hours overtime to be paid at the ordinary rate, and the second two hours at the rate of time and a half.

It was also arranged that if the meeting of the strikers, which was to take place on Friday forenoon, accept the terms, the Committees of the Men and Masters should meet on Friday afternoon to draw up and sign the document accordingly.

A Meeting of the strikers was held on Friday at 11 a.m., at the Princes Street Dramatic Club, which approved of the above conditions agreed by the Committees, but when we came to sign the document, we found that under the pretence of an alleged dissention amongst the strikers, the Masters' Committee refused to sign. We then consented to call another Meeting of the Strikers to prove their unanimity, which took place on Saturday afternoon at the Hanbury Club. The resolution of this Meeting was promptly submitted to a Meeting of Masters on Sunday night by a deputation consisting of a delegation from Manchester Executive Council of the Amalgamated Society of Tailors, of the West London District, and the Strike Committee, but they still insist in their refusal to sign the document and have therefore

BROKEN THEIR PLEDGE

agreed upon at the Conference. We therefore declare that

THE STRIKE STILL CONTINUES!!

Issued by the Tailors' Strike Committee, "White Hart," Greenfield Street, Commercial Road, Sept. 16th, 1889.

(Signed)   LEWIS LYONS, Chairman.

I. GREEN.	SILVERMAN.	DAVIS LEVY.	PHILLIP WHITE.	ALFRED LEEK.
B. COHEN.	L. GOLDSTEIN.	T. SKIDDEN.	LEWIS COHEN.	A. TENNENBAUM.
J. GOLDSTEIN.		FRIECKE.	O'CONNER.	WM. WESS, Secretary.

PENNY & HULL, PRINTERS, 53, LEMAN STREET, WHITECHAPEL, E.

CHAPTER EIGHT

CRAFTSMEN &
TRADESMEN

*The coalyard at F.B. Cameron and Co., c. 1900. Workmen are shovelling coal into sacks ready
to be loaded on to the cart. The firm had depots at 79 Bow Road and Old Ford Road.*

Costers in Spitalfields Market, 1912. Wicker baskets are stacked on shelves high above the men's heads, while crates of fruit and vegetables are waiting to be sorted on the extreme right. This traditional East End market originated in the seventeenth century. The present building dates from 1928 but due to congestion and the large numbers of lorries making deliveries, the market was moved to Temple Mills, and the building is now used as an arts and crafts market.

William Thomas Vallance, coal delivery man, at Cade's Coal Depot, Mile End. Kelly's London Post Office Trade Directory of 1928 lists Joseph Cade and Co. Coal Merchants as being located at Longnor Road, Mile End. The coal lorry is a definite improvement on the coal cart; it has a crest on the side which states 'estd 1865'.

William Thomas Vallance, coal delivery man, standing centre back row, and workmates on an outing from Cade's Coal Depot, Mile End. The lads appear to have enjoyed their outing and some on the left foreground seem a bit the worse for wear! Note they are all dressed up for the occasion, in contrast to the casual clothing people would wear for an outing such as this today.

Joseph Cade and Co. Coal Merchants, at the L&NE Railway Depot, Longnor Road, *c.* 1930. William Thomas Vallance is on the extreme right, with Robert Kidney, foremen, in the centre and William Fuller, general manager on the right of him.

A coal cart belonging to the Diamond Coal Company, *c.* 1900. The driver of the cart is being interviewed by a London City Missionary.

E. Wyatt, bedding maker, 123 Salmon Lane, *c.* 1920. The shop was run by Mrs Emily Wyatt from 1907 to 1940 and by Albert Edward Wyatt until 1955. Mattresses, bedsteads, a chaise longue and chairs are displayed outside, with a notice stating 'second-hand furniture bought'.

Another view of E. Wyatt, bedding maker, *c.* 1920. The notice reads: E. Wyatt's full size palliasse 5/6.

The office of R. Passmore and Co. in Limehouse. The company, a supplier and distributor of building materials, was founded by Robert Passmore on 5 March 1864 at 90 Three Colt Street. In 1965 the firm moved to 12 Narrow Street, and following a takeover by the Rooff Group, moved to Millwall in 1983.

R. Passmore and Co. Ltd, Lime Kiln Wharf, Three Colt Street, Limehouse, *c.* 1929. The building was part of the old Lime House, where lime was burnt, and it retained the original door and canopy, dated 1705. In the 1930s Stepney Borough carried out a slum clearance and rebuilding programme in this area, and a plaque now marks the old site in Three Colt Street.

A cooperage in Poplar High Street, said to date from Elizabethan times, viewed when it was about to be demolished. These buildings were believed to be fishermen's cottages and at one time the water came up to the backs of the dwellings.

Mr J. Cornbleet's Grocery, 71 Whitehorse Road, Stepney, 25 October 1955. Mr Cornbleet's shop was praised by the Ministry of Agriculture, Food and Fisheries as a fine example of a well-kept grocery, where all the food was wrapped or covered and a refrigerated display case held the dairy produce and meat. It was one of the many little corner shops whose livelihood and very existence came under threat with the advent of the supermarkets. The eggs prominently displayed range in price from 4½d to 6¾d a dozen.

J.H. George, bootmaker and repairer, 4 Bromley High Street, 1946. The old shoemaker's shop was near the corner of High Street Bromley and Bow Road. It dated from the seventeenth century and had a gabled and weather-boarded front. The building survived the Blitz but was demolished in February 1959.

The interior of the hairdresser's shop, 103 Old Gravel Lane, *c.* 1914. In 1919 George Warner was listed as the proprietor. It is likely that this photograph dates from the beginning of the First World War, before conscription, because the poster on the wall states: 'Your King and Country need you – join the army today!'

Albert (Bartolomeo) Faccini, piano dealer of Ernest Street, Stepney, at his barrel organ depot, *c.* 1930. An Italian by birth, Faccini came to Britain at the age of fourteen, and within a few years had acquired a barrel piano, which he hired out, at first for 1*s*, then later for 1*s* 6*d* and finally for half-a-crown. He opened his depot in Ernest Street in 1911 with five pianos. By the 1920s, when he had premises adjoining the Latimer Church, Faccini had up to thirty street pianos, which were rented out to performers unable to afford to buy an instrument. Among his customers were the Luna Boys in the 1920s, and the Nancy Boys in the 1930s. Faccini also repaired barrel organs, and had the ability to pin a new tune on a barrel. Pasquale and Company probably supplied all of Faccini's barrel pianos. On the 7 and 8 September 1940, Ernest Street suffered heavy bomb damage, and later Albert Faccini closed his business and he and his family moved to Laindon, Essex.

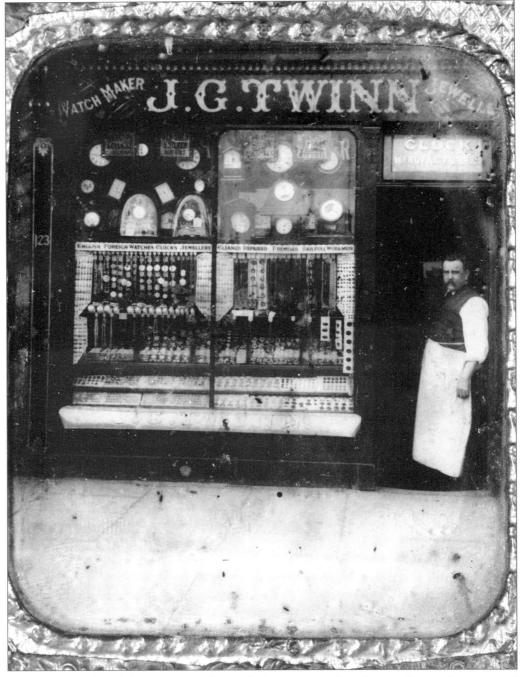

J.G. Twinn, watch and clockmakers, *c.* 1902. The business premises of James George Twinn were at 123 Mile End Road.

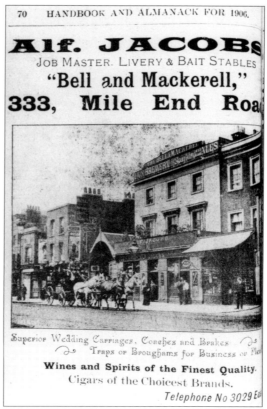

The Bell and Mackerell, 333 Mile End Road, 1906. Alfred Jacobs, Job Master (haulage contractor), set up at the Bell and Mackerell in the 1890s. In time he was joined by his sons Harry and Dave Jacobs and his nephew James. Over the years Jacobs expanded, and with the advent of the motor car the business became a car showroom and garage, with a petrol pump on the forecourt. However, they always had their carriages on display and used them for special occasions. In 1953, Dave Jacobs drove Queen Salote of Tonga in his open carriage during the coronation procession. They were also contacted by filmmakers whenever a coach and horses or carriage was required. The site of the Bell and Mackerell is now Ward Brothers Motor Spares, and Jacobs' Garage was demolished for the construction of a new building for Queen Mary and Westfield College. Harry Jacobs' son, Halifax, became famous in his own right as an East End photographer, setting up Halifax Studios in the Mile End Road.

Halifax Jacobs, photographer, Poplar, 1960s. Henry Alfred Halifax Jacobs was born on 31 March 1911 at 7 Frederick Place, Mile End, to Louisa and Harry Jacobs (son of Alfred Jacobs, Job Master at the Bell and Mackerell). Halifax was a gifted photographer, and began his career with the *East London Advertiser* after the Second World War. He had his studio and darkroom above their offices at 357 Mile End Road. A look through the *Advertiser* from the late 1940s through to the 1960s shows just how prolific he was. Halifax set up his own premises, Halifax Studios, in Mile End Road, opposite Burdett Road. Like many studios at the time, he specialized in wedding photography. He soon had studios all over the East End; one of them, Burdett Photographic, is still in existence. He died very suddenly of a heart attack outside his shop in Mile End Road on 22 June 1973.

Funeral procession of Charlie Brown, Limehouse publican, June 1932. The funeral directors were J. & D. Hannaford of 795 Commercial Road, referred to in the *East London Observer* on 11 June 1932 as 'the well known firm of Undertakers who have been established in Limehouse for over a hundred years'. In 1967 the firm was under the direction of W. Hannaford, and seems to have closed shortly afterwards. Just a few doors away from Hannaford's was another undertakers, Francis and Chris Walters, who are still doing business in Limehouse.

Funeral of Will Crooks, MP for North Woolwich, passing along East India Dock Road, by St Stephen's church, June 1921. East End funerals were and still are accompanied by all the trappings, including the funeral carriage and horses and funeral director with top hat and tails. Elaborate floral tributes are often displayed along the sides and top of the funeral cortège.

The Poplar–Bloomsbury horse tram, *c.* 1900. The side of the horse tram reads Poplar, Limehouse, Whitechapel via Commercial Street and Spitalfields Market. East London's tramway system began in 1869 when Parliament authorized the North Metropolitan Tramways Company to install over 4 miles of tramway from Whitechapel through Statford and West Ham. The Poplar–Bloomsbury horse tram began operating in 1872. The early trams had a speed limit of 9 miles per hour and running costs included supply of horseshoes at £12 a ton and the cost of keeping each horse, less than 8*s* a week. Drivers and conductors worked a sixteen-hour day, and while they were not forced to work on Sundays, they lost a day's pay if they did not. The tram line was electrified in 1906, and the last of the horse trams disappeared during the First World War, as horses were removed for war work.

The blacksmith's yard at 10 Claredale Street, Bethnal Green, September 1954. The man closest to the camera is employed on a hand-cropping machine, the other is metal cutting by oxygen (profile cutting).

Devine and Co. Whalebone Cutters, Old Ford. The firm was established in 1880 in Wrights Road and St Stephen's Road, Bow, and in the 1930s claimed to be the oldest of its kind in the country. Of their 50 or so employees, 4 had been with the firm for over 40 years and 8 for over 30 years. The bulk of the factory's produce was for the manufacture of brushes and brooms, but they also cut and prepared whalebone for belts, petershams, corsetry, surgical and scientific instruments, sports goods, fancy goods and whale ivory products, and even water divining rods.

The smithy at 10 Claredale Street, Bethnal Green, September 1954. The blacksmith is pictured working on his anvil at the forge.

A workshop of the Guild of Handicraft, Essex House, *c*. 1898. The Guild had about thirty workmen, among them W.J. Osborn, who had by then been promoted to manager of the Guild, Reinhart Read, Tom Jelliffe, Walter Curtis and A.G. Rose. Sid Cotton joined the Guild in 1896 at the age of thirteen and was a promising cabinetmaker.

The jewellery workshop, Essex House, *c.* 1898. The Guild of Handicraft was originally set up by C.R. Ashbee in Toynbee Hall, Whitechapel, in June 1888. The aim was to school ordinary East End men in the traditional skills such as cabinet making, metal work and jewellery making. The original members of the Guild were Fred Hubbard, formerly a city clerk who had artistic aspirations, John Pearson, a metalworker and skilled craftsman and designer, John Williams, an enthusiastic though unskilled metalworker, and C.V. Adams, a cabinetmaker. There was also an apprentice, Charley Atkinson.

However, Ashbee had a disagreement with Canon Barnett over the running of the school and moved the Guild to Essex House, 401 Mile End Road, almost on the corner of Grove Road. The main house was used for the Guild offices and meeting rooms, and some of the lighter metalwork was also carried out there. Permission was given for building a workshop in the garden and on 17 January 1891 Ashbee signed a twelve-year lease on the house on behalf of the Guild. On the site of Essex House there now stands Onyx House, almost opposite Mile End station.

A cabinetmaker in Shoreditch. Curtain Road and the streets adjacent in Shoreditch and Bethnal Green were the established areas for the manufacture of all kinds of furniture, and cabinetmakers took on apprentices who spent years learning the trade. Paul Martinson, a cabinetmaker, wrote a graphic account of his years of training, which was typical of the trade. He was apprenticed to a master cabinetmaker in the Hackney Road in 1930, with starting pay of 5s a week, working from 8 a.m. to 6 p.m. Mondays to Fridays and 8 a.m. to 1 p.m. on Saturdays. On Sundays he worked from 10 a.m. to 1 p.m., learning the finer skills of the trade. The company made sideboards with different shaped fronts, curved veneered doors and drawers, carved tops and claw and ball legs. All the work was done by hand. The wood was selected from one of the timber yards in the Hackney Road area and the design marked out by the cabinetmaker, who then sent the planks to the mill to be cut. The rest of the cutting, planing and shaping was done by hand, and the sections glued together in preparation for the veneer of mahogany, walnut etc. Finally the item of furniture was sent to the polishers.

R. Libling, general cabinetmakers, c. 1924. Rebecca Libling had her workshop at 72 Hare Street Bethnal Green. Standing outside the shop are Malcolm and Ray Libling, son and daughter of Rebecca Libling.

A leather worker at the East London Furniture Company (date unknown).

Master's Chair presented to the Worshipful Company of Bakers by Mr H.W. Austen Balls, proprietor of the Old George Inn, Bethnal Green. Austen Balls was Master of the Bakers' Company in 1930. He was succeeded in November 1930 by the Lord Mayor of London, Sir Phene Neal. The chair was made of English oak with the arms of the Company in heraldic design and colours on the back of the chair. The Bakers' Company awarded prizes and scholarships for baking courses at the Borough Polytechnic.

CHAPTER NINE

WORKING FOR SURVIVAL

Professional photographer Ted Swinford, in the bowler hat, prepares to photograph a family in their back yard at 63 Viaduct Street, c. 1940. Street photographers went from house to house, encouraging families to have their photographs taken. During the Second World War Swinford was employed with Bethnal Green Council as a fuel overseer.

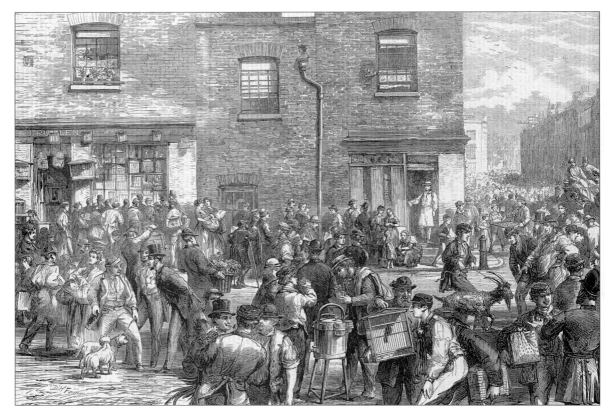

The Sunday morning Bird Fair in Club Row, Bethnal Green, *Illustrated Times*, 8 August 1868. The scene is on the corner of Club Row and Anchor Street. Animals and birds are being touted for sale, on the right is a boy with a goat, while in the extreme right foreground, a policeman is questioning a young man. In the background J. Pullen has cages of all sizes hanging up in his shop, and in the left foreground is a good likeness of Bill Sykes and his bulldog in conversation with a gentleman in a top hat.

The article states:

For the last 25 years or more Club Row, Shoreditch, and the neighbourhood, have been rendered somewhat notorious by the Sunday morning bird fair held in that quarter. Here, from about 10.30 am up to 1.30 pm every Sunday are congregated men and lads from all parts of the metropolis: some with birds, canaries, linnets etc others with pigeons, fowls, dogs, white mice and so on. Now and then may be seen a goat, and horses and ponies are occcasionally trotted up and down to show their paces. Here may frequently be found the strangest collection of artificial living birds exhibited in the universe. Birds that would puzzle Buffon as to species, of brilliant plumage, and wonderful topknots, that drop off in the most marvellous manner in a very short space of time; sparrows and linnets transformed into canaries, sporting a brand new coat of yellow; and extraordinary specimens of the feathered tribe caught a few hours previously on Hackney marshes one of which perhaps, by a swift change of nationality, comes out unblushingly as a 'beautiful thing, sir, just brought over by a sailor from Timbuctoo or Constantinople. And I'll sell it to you sir, for 5*s* 7*d* although Jack told me solemnly not to take less than a half a guinea'. Incredulous as it may appear there are persons gullible enough to believe the story and hand over the 5*s* 7*d* for a spotted sparrow.

A young lad sits waiting hopefully with shoe-shining equipment opposite Aldgate station, July 1899. The shoeblacks venture began on 31 March 1851, during the Great Exhibition, as a means of finding employment for young lads from the Ragged Schools. The boys from the brigades organized by the Ragged School Union were given uniforms to wear and the various brigades could be recognized by their colours. At the Central Brigade the boys were expected to hand over all their day's earnings to the superintendent, who gave them 6d for the day's work. The remaining money was divided into three parts. One third was kept by the society, one third given back to the boy and the final third put into a bank account for the boy. Brigade Inspectors went around checking on the shoeblacks to make sure they remained hard at work, and did not idle their time away. Some brigades charged rent for the 'station' and deducted a proportion of earnings for meals and lodgings. A cup of coffee and two pieces of bread could cost 1d, with 3d for a bed for the night. Work started at 6.30 a.m. in summer and 7.15 a.m. in winter and the boys finished work at 6.30 p.m. On returning to the home, they booked their money, washed, had tea and then did lessons for an hour. Supper was from 7 to 8 p.m., and the boys had to be in bed by 10.30 p.m.

In the background 19, 20 and 21 Aldgate High Street, on the north side, are seen, while on the right is a road worker with his cart.

A yard in Bethnal Green, *c.* 1900. Scrapwood is being turned into firewood for sale to East End households for a few pence.

The Cat's Meat Man, 1902. A familiar sight in the East End, this tradesman made his living by selling cooked offal from house to house. The decorative lettering 'E R' above the doorway appears to be celebrating the coronation of Edward VII in 1902.

One of C.R. Ashbee's first recruits into the Guild of Handicraft was Bill Hardiman who used to earn 15s a week selling cat's meat from a barrow in Whitechapel, considered a well-paid job by East End standards. However, Ashbee saw in him the essence of what the Guild was all about, turning ordinary working men with no experience in the arts and crafts into skilled artisans.

In the 1920s a worker for the People's Dispensary for Sick Animals described how she came upon a cat's meat barrow in the East End, where women were picking over the contents, and deciding on a 'pennorth for Bob' and 'a ha'porth for Nell'. One of the prospective customers advised her that 'you get more if yer 'as knobs, but it all depends on what you want it for'. When times were hard, it was not unknown for wives to serve cat's meat to their unsuspecting husbands for tea!

An ice-cream vendor in Grundy Street, *c.* 1930. With open boxes of cones at one end, the ice-cream seller is dispensing his wares from one of two pails, and to his left is a slop bucket. The little girl in the foreground impatiently waits for service, clutching her penny.

The knife-grinder in East India Dock Road, *c.* 1930. This photograph appears to have been taken from the upper window of William Whiffin's photographic studio, which faced the corner of Cotton Street with East India Dock Road.

Making streamers at home, early 1900s. This photograph was taken by the Salvation Army to publicize its work in the East End of London among the poorest families. This family survived by making paper streamers for decorations and celebrations.

National Savings Campaign procession held in Bethnal Green, Saturday 27 September 1947. This campaign was a postwar government initiative to encourage people to save and invest. A Rag and Bone man's cart drives past Bethnal Green Town Hall, Cambridge Heath Road.

A sketch of the Bird Mart in the East End, the *Graphic*, 25 December 1869. Birds and animals of all description were sold in Club Row and the streets adjacent to Brick Lane and Bethnal Green Road. A sailor is extolling the virtues of his cockatoo, while another holds a small dog. In the foreground a young lad holds a cockerel and leads a goat. This was a familiar scene as late as the mid-twentieth century.

Opposite: A young girl is making sacks between school hours to earn extra income for the family, *c.* 1899. She is using her sewing skills to stitch coarse sacking. The pictures on this page represent the bottom end of the rag trade. Workers collected their strips of sacking, but had to use their own needles and twine. The work was hard and very rough on the hands.

The caption for this picture from the *Illustrated London News* reads: 'Sackmaking in the East End of London, No. 8 Rahn's Court, Shadwell'. Rahn's Court was, in fact, not in Shadwell but was a tiny turning off Back Church Lane, between Ellen Street and Pinchin Street in Whitechapel. However, it is a bleak depiction of poverty in the East End, where whole families engaged in the desperate struggle for survival, working long hours into the night to earn a few pennies to pay the rent and perhaps buy a loaf of bread.

P. Capaldi's ice-cream cart, *c.* 1920. Italian ice-cream vendors made their own ice-cream and sold it from brightly painted barrows, which held two drum-shaped containers, one holding proper ice-cream and the other water ice. Both were served with a wooden scoop and put on to paper squares, which were held in the hand, while the ice cream was licked off! Water ice, or sorbet, cost ½d and was served with a wedge of lemon. The ice-cream van was one of the most welcome sights on the streets in summer.

Brushmaking at home in the East End. An unknown woman sits making brushes with the help of her young daughter, while the other daughter takes care of the youngest child. Three little boys sit wearily on the bedstead, awaiting their mother's attention. The woman is fixing the bristles into the base of the brush, with the wooden backs of the brushes on her left. The bare wooden floor and the children's apparel are indicative of the family's poverty.

CHAPTER TEN

FOOD PRODUCTION

Allen & Hanbury's factory in Bethnal Green, 1927. These women are working at conveyor belts in the food weighing and packing department. Besides medical equipment and pharmaceuticals, the factory also produced milk foods, syrups, malt extracts and baby foods.

The East End had hundreds of factories turning out processed food for mass consumption, and thousands of men and women found employment at these factories – Morton's jams, preserves and confectioneries and Mcdougall's Flour Mills were on the Isle of Dogs; Bromley and Bow had the Sun Flour Mills and the Far Famed Cake Company as well as the famous Spratt's Dog Biscuit manufacturers; Clarke, Nicholls and Coombs (Clarnicos), the confectionery company was just north of Bow. These were just a few of the household names, familiar to many.

There were bakeries on almost every street, baking and selling bread, the staple food of the working class. At the beginning of the century there were ninety-three basement bakehouses in the Stepney area alone, of which only sixty-nine were granted certificates of suitability under the Factory and Workshops Act of 1901. At the commencement of the Factory and Workshops Act of 1937 there were still thirty-three basement bakehouses in the borough. By 1946 this number had been reduced to twenty, partly by bombing and other disturbances during the war. In 1949 eleven of the remaining basement bakehouses in Stepney were given three years' notice to close.

During the 1800s London's population increased rapidly and the dairy trade grew along with it. By 1861, 72 per cent of London's milk came from town cowsheds and the number of cattle peaked at 24,000. Dairies, often no more than a few cows in the backyard of a terrace house, sold fresh milk twice a day. Cowsheds were not properly built or ventilated, little attention was paid to hygiene and the milk supplied was of dubious quality. One estimate says there were up to four pints of water to every ten of milk. The cow with the iron tail – the water pump – was acknowledged to be of prime importance in supplying London with milk!

But the increasing population and new hygiene regulations served to squeeze out the cowkeepers. The 597 cowhouses in the late 1800s had become 180 by 1912, and the total dairy cow population had dropped to less than 2,500. This rate accelerated during and after the First World War, but probably the biggest factor of all which ended the East End cowkeeper was the price war of the 1930s. London cowkeepers had always charged slightly more than normal for fresh milk, but in the 1930s about 500 street traders sold milk at 4d to 5d a quart compared to the cowkeepers' 6d to 7d.

The main distribution centre for fruit and vegetables was Spitalfields Market. A market stood on this site for centuries, first founded by charter in 1682. The present buildings date from 1928, when the market was enlarged and modernized. The streets surrounding the market thronged with life from the early hours of the morning to late at night. Those who could bought the best, those who could not foraged in the bins for what was thrown away.

For the majority of households in East London the daily trip to the corner grocer was a necessary routine. Women did their shopping late in the evening and shops would stay open until 8 p.m. or later. Their shopping list would include a 1d scoop of jam, a 1d packet of tea, a ½ lb of sugar and a 2½d tin of condensed milk. Meat was a luxury, bought from the local butcher, served as a Sunday joint if the family could afford it and eked out for the rest of the week, with bread and potatoes being the mainstay of the family diet.

Stones used in grinding Allinson wholemeal flour at the Natural Food Co. Ltd, Bethnal Green, *c.* 1912. At 21a Patriot Square the company took over the Cyclone Flour and Meal Company, based there since about 1895. New and imposing offices fronting 210–15 Cambridge Road were built later and the firm became the largest wholemeal milling company in the country. By 1911 about 11 million loaves were made by them annually. Allinsons claimed that their method of grinding wheat the traditional way between millstones, as opposed to steel rollers, was proven to be beneficial to health and contributed to the prevention of constipation. The company also claimed that their wholewheat flour retained more of the essential minerals and nutrients, and was made from pure wheat, which had nothing added and nothing taken away. The Bethnal Green factory closed in 1971 when the multi-national company Booker-McConnell took over.

J.F. List, baker, 418 Bethnal Green Road, 2 October 1906. The directory of 1908 states that Philip Frederick List was the proprietor. The window advertises the shop as being 'special baker of Dr Allinson's bread, by appointment'. From the 1880s to the early 1900s Dr Allinson, a highly successful dietician who advocated wholemeal bread at every meal, issued personal testimonial certificates of wholemeal bread quality to complying bakers.

The Sun Flour Mills, Bromley by Bow, *c.* 1910. On the right can be seen part of Walmsley's Maltings, which were demolished by the LCC in 1934. In May 1952 the Sun Flour Mills were partially destroyed by a major fire, which burned for more than two hours.

Fish curing, Limehouse, 1936. Fish, such as salmon, was first gutted, then filleted and covered with salt for a few hours. The filleted fish was then strung up on poles to be hung in the smoke hole. There were numerous complaints to the health inspectors from the residents adjoining the fish curers. Fish offal was often left lying around in open tubs before being disposed of, and the smell was abominable. Mr J.F. Johnson of Bow Common Lane, who collected fish offal for conversion into manure, used vans with air-tight tanks for collection, which the council approved of, and every fish curer was supplied with one of Mr Johnson's tanks. However, not all the fish curers used them and many continued with the old system of carrying the offal through the streets in open carts.

Fish curing, Limehouse, 1930. In the final process, the cured, dried fish is packed away; the tables are covered with newspaper to protect the fish. Benjamin Hughes, wearing the cap, passes the cured fish to Johnny Warren at the counter. Benjamin Hughes was the third generation of the same family to become a fish curer at Limehouse. The Hughes family lived at 175 Eastfield Street. The fish smoke holes were at 185 Eastfield Street.

P. Lowry, dried fish shop, 22–4 Brick Lane, c. 1895. The dried fish, as seen in the previous two photographs, are displayed for sale still attached to the poles or skewers on which they were cured.

Cave Brothers, cowkeepers, 42 Jubilee Street, Stepney, 1938. Mr and Mrs Cave ran their small farm in the heart of Stepney, just off the Commercial Road, supplying milk to the neighbourhood. They had forty-five cows and three horses, as well as chickens, ducks and even rabbits. The Cave family had farmed here for four generations, and were apparently very successful. They could obtain fodder relatively cheaply, with the local breweries providing brewers grain, Spitalfields Market the vegetables, and Whitechapel hay market (which closed in 1928) close by. There was little competition from commercial dairies, as the local people could only afford to buy in small quantities.

Although Stepney had more cowsheds than any other borough in London, by 1936 there were only 36 cowkeepers, who had 151 cows between them, and this declined to 19 in 1938. Just 2 years later there were 16 left and by 1950 only 2.

A Weller's Table Water delivery van, *c.* 1925. In 1930 Mrs Alice Harriet Weller was listed as a confectioner at 73 Virginia Road, Bethnal Green, and mineral-water manufacturer at 17 Cottrill Road, Hackney.

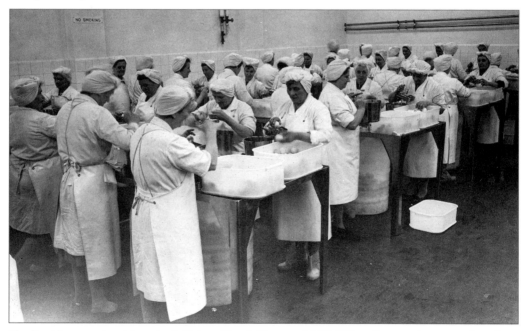

The liquid egg pasteurizing plant, Nelson Street, Stepney, 1963. When the new law came into force regarding pasteurization, a firm of egg merchants in Nelson Street installed an egg pasteurization plant in a purpose-built factory. They employed fifty women in an air-conditioned, insect-proof room, to break eggs one by one, smell them and look for defects such as blood spots etc. Bad eggs were discarded into a bin, and the good broken eggs were then passed through a stainless-steel filter to eliminate bits of shell, until finally the liquid egg was poured into tanks holding 2,000 gallons, or into 28 lb tins.

CHAPTER ELEVEN

BREWERIES & PUBLIC HOUSES

The Maltings, Bromley by Bow, 1934. The Walmsley's Maltings, where malt was made for a hundred years, were purchased by the London County Council in 1934 and later demolished. The Coventry Cross Estate now occupies this site.

An illustration of Truman's Brewery in Hanbury Street, *c.* 1780. Breweries were an established trade in the East End from at least the sixteenth century. Early breweries were situated by the River Lea, which provided the water for the manufacturing process. The three major breweries in the East End were Truman Hanbury Buxton & Co. Ltd in Spitalfields, Mann, Crossman and Paulin's Albion Brewery in Whitechapel and Charrington's Anchor Brewery in the Mile End Road. The brewery of Messrs Truman, Hanbury Buxton & Co. in Spitalfields was one of the oldest in London, having been established in 1666, the year of the Great Fire of London. Thomas Bucknall set up a brewery in a field at Spittlehope, now Spitalfields, and he was soon to be joined by Joseph Truman, who was known as a brewer in Brick Lane from at least 1674. In 1690 Benjamin Truman was born in Brick Lane and by 1760 he was head of Truman's Brewery. It was during this time that the brewery became famous for its production of 'Porter', a black stout that could be brewed in large quantities without deterioration. He was later knighted for services to London in general and to Spitalfields in particular. A notable event in the history of the firm occurred in 1737, when the Prince of Wales caused a bonfire to be lit and free beer to celebrate the birth of the Duchess of Brunswick. The beer was of such poor quality that the crowd rioted. The next day, to pacify the discontented populace, the Prince ordered four barrels from Truman's in Brick Lane, which was pronounced to be of the highest quality, to be distributed among the crowds gathered outside Carlton House, London. Another name was added to the title of the firm when Sampson Hanbury joined the brewery in 1789 and finally in 1808, Thomas Buxton joined Truman's. It was made a limited company in 1889. The brewery enlarged and extended its premises at Brick Lane to both sides of the road, but was taken over by Grand Met in the 1990s, and eventually closed.

The Brunswick Tap at Blackwall, 1849. This painting by H.R. Allen shows the departure of Messrs Green's frigate *Malacca* bound for Bombay from Brunswick Pier on the 26 December 1849. The inn later became the Railway Tavern before being converted into the Dockmaster's House. In 1928 a plaque was placed on the wall of the building commemorating the departure of the Virginia Settlers from Blackwall in December 1606.

The Old George public house, 379 Bethnal Green Road, 1885. The proprietor is Harry J. Balls. The barrels lining the pavement have presumably been placed there for the purpose of the photograph, and along with the proprietor, the drayman and the potmen, the entire street appears to have turned out to be featured in the picture, including a policeman standing by the shop to the left.

Anchor Brewery of Charrington & Co. in the Mile End Road. This brewery was established here in 1757 and replaced the Bethnal Green brewery of Westfield and Moss, of which John Charrington was a partner. In 1783 John Charrington and his brother Harry became the proprietors. In 1833 Charrington's absorbed the firm of Steward and Head, and began brewing stout and porter instead of just ale. Charrington's bought Savill's Brewery in Stratford in 1925. At about the same time, the Abbey Brewery at Burton was closed and bitter was brewed at Mile End. In 1929 Seabrooke's Brewery at Grays Essex was added to the company, and in 1933 Hoare's Brewery was purchased. In 1953 Charrington entered into an agreement with Canada Dry International to bottle and market their products. Anchor Brewery was rebuilt in 1977 and an extensive new block was added; these new buildings were opened in August 1978. Charrington's Brewery finally closed in 1994.

Opposite: Firemen attending to their equipment in the firefighting department of Charrington's Brewery, *c.* 1930. The danger of fire was ever-present and over the years there were several major fires in East End factories in the 1920s and 1930s, including one at Charrington's.

A pen and grey ink sketch of Charrington's Anchor Brewery in the Mile End Road, nineteenth century. By this time the brewery was solely owned by John and Harry Charrington. In 1808 they came second on the list of the leading twelve London Brewers, producing 20,252 barrels a year. The brewery stood in what was then the pleasant hamlet of Mile End Old Town. Around the building were gardens and open fields and just up the road was the toll gate. John Charrington bought the 16 acres lying just behind the site of the modern brewery and made it into a park, building on it a house of a generous size which used to be the home of the senior partner and his family. But with the expansion of the brewery the family left and the house was demolished. Part of the remaining ground was given to St Peter's church. By the middle of the nineteenth century there were about eighty brewery horses and by the 1890s the number had doubled. Horses were used until the end of the Second World War, when all the brewery's transport was mechanized and to the regret of many the last horse was sold in 1946.

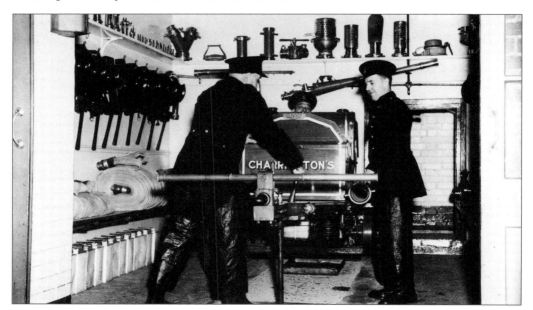

The interior of the Prospect of Whitby, Wapping, one of the oldest inns in London, *c.* 1959. Now one of the most popular tourist pubs in the Docklands area, the Prospect has come a long way since it's establishment as a waterfront tavern. Photographs taken inside pubs are not common.

The ritual of hanging up a hot cross bun, an annual Good Friday event, performed by a sailor at the Widow's Son pub in Devon's Road, Bromley by Bow, March 1964. Mr John Jackson, from HMS *Mercury*, adds another bun to the bag hanging from the ceiling in the pub. The Widow's Son was also known as the Bun House, and it is said that a widow lived here with her sailor son. In anticipation of his return after a long spell at sea, she baked him a hot cross bun for Good Friday. Sadly, the young sailor's ship was lost in a storm at sea, but his mother never gave up hope of seeing him again, and every year without fail she would bake a hot cross bun for him. This tradition still continues, and every year a sailor is invited to hang a fresh bun from the ceiling.

The City Arms, Bromley by Bow, *c.* 1904. This pub was at 134 Devon's Road, on the corner of Reeves Road. While the proprietor, W. Zimmermann, and his family and employees have arranged themselves outside the pub, in Reeves Road on the right four street sweepers also pose with their brooms, and a man pushing a barrow in Devon's Road enters the frame on the left.

Cleaning up in a pub after the floods in Orchard Place, Bow Creek, January 1928. In the early hours of Saturday 8 January the flood which swept in on the high tide from the North Sea descended on Poplar like a wall of water, carrying devastation to hundreds of small homes which were inundated with 4 to 5 ft of water. In an attempt to release the water at Orchard House, Blackwall, a diver was sent down to open a submerged sluice. There were several accidents as a result, the most serious being when the boat accompanying the diver and rescuers was upset trapping the diver, who had to be rescued and was badly injured and admitted to Poplar Hospital. When the flood water finally subsided it left behind a thick oily sludge, which ruined household goods and rendered houses almost uninhabitable.

CHAPTER TWELVE

COUNCIL WORKERS & THE PUBLIC SECTOR

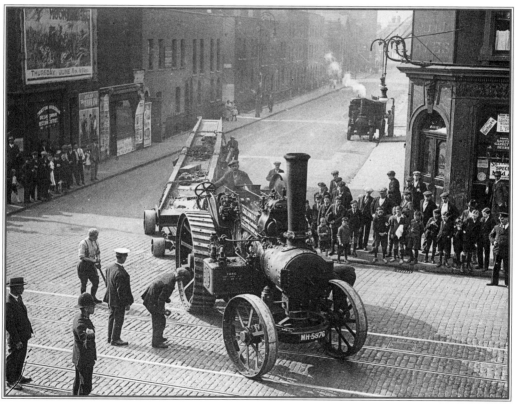

A crowd gathers to watch a steam traction engine in Cotton Street, on the corner with East India Dock Road, Poplar, c. 1928. In the background is a Poplar Borough Council steam watering vehicle.

The three metropolitan boroughs of Stepney, Bethnal Green and Poplar, formed in 1900, were among the poorest boroughs of London. High unemployment, overcrowding in slum tenements, the heavy pollution of the area by local manufacturers and bad practice by small traders, who constantly flouted the health and saftey regulations, meant a heavy work load for the health inspectors and the sanitary department.

Following a landslide Labour victory after the First World War, Poplar Council fought hard for two years to bring about a change in the way rates were levied by the London County Council, arguing that Poplar, the poorest borough, was forced to levy the highest rates, while Westminster, for instance, with very few seeking poor relief, levied the lowest rates. The government refused to address the issue and Poplar Council responded by reducing its rates and refusing to pay its share of the London County Council, police, fire and Metropolitan Asylum contributions. After several threats were made by the LCC, Poplar Council was eventually summoned to court. After George Lansbury had appealed to the people to support their councillors, a crowd of over 2,000 marched with them. They were led by the deputy mayor, Charlie Sumner, and accompanied by a drum and fife band, as well as the dockers', vehicle workers' and general workers' trade unions. Many had given up a day's work to join the protest. Despite their strong arguments and appeals, thirty councillors were sentenced to six weeks' imprisonment. On 3 September 1921, the councillors were arrested, the men taken to Brixton prison and the five women councillors and aldermen were imprisoned at Holloway. Their six-week stay in prison did achieve a result, however, and eventually the law was amended to rationalize rates across London.

Shortly after this, having highlighted the East End's endemic shortage of housing and often appalling living conditions, a scheme was devised by the London County Council to rehouse thousands of East Enders at the Becontree housing development. This plan was carried through into the 1930s, while at the same time Stepney embarked on an ambitious slum-clearance scheme, which met with fierce opposition in some neighbourhoods. Annie Barnes, a Stepney councillor who was on the housing committee, described the opposition to the scheme when the first slums in Wapping were selected for demolition and rebuilding. The people were to be rehoused in the empty Strangers' Homes in West India Dock Road. This building, used as lodgings for Lascars from 1857, had been closed down because of lack of use. But when the architect and borough engineer paid a visit to the neighbourhood, they were attacked with broomsticks and choppers and had to call for police protection. Bethnal Green's efforts to improve living conditions can be witnessed today in the Boundary Estate, and later in Cranbrook Estate.

Stepney was the centre of the food trade. The docks handled large imports of food and there were major wholesale markets, such as Spitalfields, and several large food factories in the borough. Dr F. Roantree O'Shiel, Medical Officer of Health in Stepney from 1937, noted in his report for 1952: 'Byelaws for the clean handling of food came into force on 3rd November 1952. These byelaws not only cover shops and cafés but also the sale of food in the open-air. In the latter case they are difficult to apply. It is quite impossible to equip food-barrows with hot and cold water and proper sanitary conditions and no amount of care can keep dust and flies from food sold under such primitive conditions. With the multiplicity of well-equipped food shops in 1952, barrows and snack shacks would seem unnecessary but ancient customs die hard.'

The Second World War put a tremendous strain on the three boroughs' resources. Heavy bombardment reduced large sections of the East End to rubble, as planes targeted the docks. However, following the war and the reduction in the population of the area, partly due to the evacuation process, by 1964 it was clearly no longer viable to have three separate boroughs and in 1965 they amalgamated to form the London Borough of Tower Hamlets.

Poplar councillors and aldermen marching down East India Dock Road, Friday 29 July 1921. This photograph was taken during the Poplar Rates dispute and the men are on their way to the Law Courts in the Strand.

Mr E.S. Bossley, Mace Bearer and Hall Keeper for Poplar Borough Council, photographed to celebrate thirty-five years of service, 4 May 1934.

Mr Bernard Lewis, librarian, in the Stepney Central Library, c. 1950. Bernard Lewis was born in Bethnal Green and started work at Whitechapel Library at the age of sixteen as a junior assistant. He was in charge of Stepney Local History Collection for eighteen years, after which he was made Area Librarian in charge of Whitechapel, St George's in the East and Wapping, before retiring in April 1973, having worked for the library service for forty-four years.

Stepney Central Library, 1960. Miss S. Pringle, the librarian, deals with a borrower in the lending library at Bancroft Road, Mile End.

Building work in Stepney, 1937. In 1934 Stepney embarked on an ambitious programme of slum clearance and rebuilding. Whole streets of mean tenements were swept away to be replaced by solidly constructed blocks of flats. However, the advent of war in 1939 brought all rebuilding work to a halt.

Orlit Houses under construction in Ada Gardens, Blair Street, Poplar, 1945. These experimental prefabricated houses were erected by the council in response to the pressing need for suitable accommodation as part of the post-war rebuilding programme in the borough. They were manufactured by Orlit Ltd of Buckingham Gate, and consisted of a structural precast concrete frame, clad in small precast reinforced concrete panels, with cavity external walls and a flat roof. These houses were built by the borough's own direct labour force. In January 1946 Mrs Eleanor Roosevelt paid a visit to Poplar and inspected the Orlits.

Imported canned meats are checked by the public health inspector and council food inspectors at Free Trade Wharf, 1952. The foreman is breaking open cases containing the cans of Vienna sausages, which are scrutinized by the public health inspector. The man in the centre of the picture, wearing an improvised sack apron, does not look particularly happy at being involved in the process.

Inspection of a butter-blending factory by Stepney Borough Council, 1952. The public health inspector is in the process of testing a sample of butter, under the Food and Drugs Act of 1938. There were thirty-four butter and margarine factories in the borough and during the year twenty-eight inspections were made. In 1955 there were thirty-one factories and forty inspections made, although only one factory was served with notice to close.

Old Poplar Baths, East India Dock Road. In the foreground can been seen the barrow of some street cleaners, one of whom is pushing a broom on the right. The baths were built in 1851, and opened on 24 July 1852. They were later enlarged in 1886 but closed in 1931, were entirely rebuilt and reopened on Saturday 20 January 1934. The baths contained first- and second-class swimming pools, slipper baths, vapour baths and steam rooms, and laundries for washing and drying clothes. The first Public Baths and Washhouses Act was passed in 1846, and Poplar Baths was one of the first to be built after this. They were an essential part of life in Poplar, where many houses had no bathrooms or facilities for bathing. The council also encouraged women to use the laundry services provided in an attempt to discourage washing at home, where damp clothing would remain hanging up inside for days. Use of the baths and the swimming pool was strictly segregated by sex. The prohibition on mixed bathing was lifted in 1925, although this was only allowed in LCC's parks in 1927. On 29 September 1933 Poplar Council advertised for an assistant superintendent (male) at Poplar Baths – 'For new baths to be opened shortly – salary payable £250 per annum with increments of £25 to a maximum of £300 per annum.' In 1939 Poplar Council debated on whether to allow men to wear trunks during mixed bathing, but decided that they should wear a full costume so as not to offend the ladies.

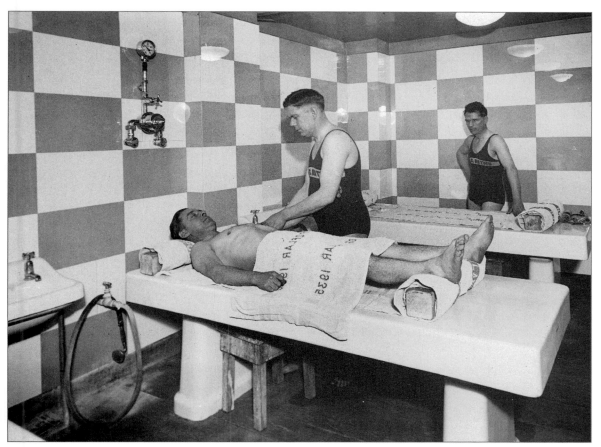

The massage room in the vapour baths at the Poplar Baths, 1935. Foam baths and Russian vapour baths, with a massage by a professional masseur, were offered, as well as a much advertised 'Zotofoam sweating bath', said to be invaluable in the treatment of all rheumatic pains. In 1936, a report on the Baths stated: 'Here for an extra sixpence, or in the case of pine baths, one shilling sixpence, one can have special baths and massage at the hands of experts.'

In October 1934, the baths and washhouses committee of the Poplar Borough Council reported that requests had been made by patrons of the vapour section at Poplar Baths for cologne-friction massage and that medicated bath salts should be available in the slipper-bath section. The committee therefore recommended that cologne friction be introduced at a charge of 1s and medicated bath salts, sufficient for one bath, be supplied at 2d a carton.

Workers digging up the pavements in Ford Street, Bow, 1945. Second on left is Jack who lived in Bethnal Green. Next to him was another Irish labourer, all mates of Harry Willmott.

Harry Willmott on the left, at 3 Ford Street, Bow, 1945. This picture shows Jack with his hat on. The photographs on this page were taken with an old box camera of 1920s vintage.

East End police men who were part of the police strike, August 1919. This was the second strike by London's police force, following the government's refusal to allow them to form a union. In 1913 the Police and Prison Officers' Union was formed by ex-Inspector Symes and in 1917 it was reorganized, without securing either recognition or sanction. Following several instances of victimization, there was a sudden strike by London's police force on 29 August 1918. The situation was defused by the Prime Minister Lloyd George, who promised their leader that there would be improvements, but only after the cessation of hostilities.

On 31 July 1919, a second strike was suddenly called, which resulted in failure and only a couple of thousand men coming out in London and a few hundred in Liverpool, Birkenhead and elsewhere, together with a small number of prison warders. The Home Secretary refused to recognize a trade union in the police force and prison staff and all the strikers were sacked. The government, however, did announce large concessions regarding wages, promotion, pensions and agreed to the establishment of an elective organization of the police force, with each grade having a representative on the committee, through whom they could make formal representations and complaints. These measures were embodied in the Police Act, 1919, which explicitly prohibited the police from becoming either members of or being affiliated to any trade union or political organization.

The eight defiant policemen seen here who refused to compromise piled their blue uniforms and helmets on to a coster's barrow and wheeled it to Poplar police station, where they handed them in. The authorities moved swiftly and savagely to ensure that there was no further disruption. None of the 1,083 London police men who went on strike were ever reinstated and all lost their pension rights.

Inspector Stocks, inspector of police for the East and West India Dock Company, *c.* 1890. The 1881 census shows Henry Stocks, age thirty-one, dock constable, living at 9 Leamouth Place with his wife Elizabeth and daughters Elizabeth, 10, Esther, 7, Henrietta, 5, and Maryann, 1 year old. As the latter two were born in Blackwall, Henry Stocks must have been residing at Blackwall for at least five years. There were several other dock constables living at Leamouth Place, including Richard Moore, Michael Flynn, Craigg Brown and Frederick Kitchen.

The army recruiting office, 156 East India Dock Road, 1914. The building was adjacent to Poplar recreation park. The caption on the bus reads: 'To Berlin and Back Free'.

The drawing office, Poplar Borough Council, *c.* 1937. Photographs of the interior of the council office are extremely rare.

Home Guards marching past Bethnal Green gardens during the Second World War.

Fire watching from the roof of the Troxy Cinema Commercial Road, Stepney, during the Second World War. The Troxy opened in 1933 with the film *King Kong*. The theatre later became the London Opera Centre and in 1994 was transformed into a bingo hall.

F Post at fire practice, Wilmot Street, Bethnal Green, 1939. The Council put out an 'Urgent Appeal to Women Citizens – Volunteers are required for Civil Defence in your Borough as Air Raid Wardens, First Aid Workers, help in evacuation of children, Canteen Workers, Auxiliary nurses, Clerical workers, telephonists and Hospital supply workers'. The Mayoress of Bethnal Green, Mrs Edwards, who is on the extreme right, wearing a white blouse, offers encouragement to a few of the volunteers who had responded to the Council's advertisement. Two of the volunteers are Mrs D. Lloyd and Anne Smith.

Trench digging at Poplar recreation ground, during the phoney war, before the crisis of 1938. The area the men are digging in is where the present tennis courts are. Many thousands of men were engaged on ARP trench digging, before the 'go easy' order was issued. On 29 July 1938 Poplar Council submitted a scheme for trench shelter accommodation in the parks, to hold 9,610 people. It was estimated that it would take 6,970 men five days to complete the work in all the borough's parks. The trenches excavated were approximately 4 ft 6 in deep and lined with sandbags, the trenches being 20 ft apart built with traverses with two 15-ft seating recesses in each traverse. The trenches were to be covered with corrugated-iron sheeting and sandbags. 875 men were required for work in Poplar Recreation Park. John Maguire was one of the many who participated in the trench digging at Millwall and Poplar recreation grounds in September 1938. On 1 October 1938 the men were informed that their services were no longer required, and they were paid off. However, it took several days for their cards to be returned, during which time they were unable to seek employment.

Bow Road. Workers protecting Poplar Town Hall with sandbags. The town hall is on the corner of Bow Road and Fairfield Road and in the distance on the left can be seen the Bow memorial fountain, which was demolished in the 1960s.

The construction of an air-raid shelter at Sumner House, Maddams Street, Bromley, 1939. On the right sandbags are waiting to be filled. Poplar Council estimated that 3,608,000 sandbags were required for the borough's Civil Defence preparations. The cost to Poplar for trench digging was £38,366, with air-raid precautions estimated at £4,500, and 'sandbagging offices' a mere £72!

Rip, the ARP dog, helps the Post warden E. King search for people buried under debris. A little short-legged dog with a stout body of no particular breed, and reckoned to be six or seven years old, he was found by Post Warden E. King of Civil Defence Squad, Post B at 132 Southill Street, Poplar, after a heavy raid in 1940 and he was immediately adopted by the Post. He proved to be an invaluable asset in their work and was awarded the Dickin Medal 'for locating many air-raid victims buried by rubble during the blitz of 1940'.

The Dickin Medal, instituted by Maria Elizabeth Dickin (Founder of the People's Dispensary for Sick Animals) and popularly referred to as 'the animals VC', was awarded to any animal that displayed conspicuous gallantry and devotion to duty associated with or under the control of any branch of the armed forces or Civil Defence units during the Second World War and its aftermath. Rip was one of only eighteen dogs to receive this award.

In the aftermath of a bombing raid during the Second World War, ARP men come to the rescue, searching the ruins of a house for survivors.

CHAPTER THIRTEEN

WASTE DISPOSAL & SANITATION

Inspection of the Borough of Stepney's refuse carts by an unknown lady. Her elegant clothes and fox fur are in stark contrast to the dustman she is observing, as he empties his load from a tin bath into the cart.

The following selection of pictures shows the progress of sanitation, rubbish collection and disposal through one hundred years, from the construction of Bazalgette's drainage system and the methods of waste disposal employed by the boroughs to the main waste disposal plant at Northumberland Wharf in Poplar. The latter unit gained considerable attention during the Second World War when the borough launched a major campaign to recycle everything possible for the war effort. The enthusiasm with which the East End replied can be gauged by the photographs taken at the time, showing the enormous response and the incredible variety of items collected.

Up to the mid-nineteenth century the River Thames was highly polluted, with all of London's sewers flowing directly into it. During the hot summer of 1859, 4,281 tons of chalk lime, 478 tons of chloride of lime, and 50 tons of carbolic acid were poured into the Thames to suppress the noxious odours arising from the river. After a succession of cholera epidemics, the government was forced to address the question of proper drainage and sanitation and Joseph Bazalgette, appointed Chief Engineer to the Metropolitan Board of Works on 25 January 1856, was given the task of sorting out London's drainage problems. In 1858 Bazalgette began his gigantic works for providing the whole of London, both north and south of the river, with a properly planned main drainage system. *The Times* of 18 August 1873 proclaimed that 'London has been transformed in a comparatively brief period, if not into a clean, at least into a healthy city'. The completion of this monumental task effectivly put an end to the cholera outbreaks which periodically swept through the East End of London. The main sewers, high, middle and low on both sides of the river, converged on outfall sewers running to reservoirs some 26 miles below London Bridge, at Crossness and Beckton. There is a public path from Stratford via Plaistow along the northern outfall sewer.

Bazalgette's drainage system under construction, 1859. This illustration shows the brickwork of the tunnels near Old Ford, Bow.

Construction of the metropolitan high-level sewer, near Victoria Park, part of Bazalgette's drainage system, 1859. Our picture shows workmen busily engaged in digging and carrying away the spoil from the trench.

Whitechapel dustmen with cart in Old Montague Street, 1895. This picture is from the collection of the Revd Cecil Cohen, curate of Whitechapel from 1912 to 1915. The Commodore public house is in the background and Jacob Nyman ran the corn chandler's shop on the right, at 40 Old Montague Street.

Bales of waste material being loaded on to a barge for transportation down the Thames.

A Stepney Borough Council engineer
inspects the drains, 1956.

A council employee collecting waste food for feeding pigs, *c.* 1945. The collection of waste food products began during the Second World War, and continued right up to September 1955. The work would have been quite arduous, going from house to house and knocking at every door. The waste food was collected and delivered on a daily basis to a concentrator plant in Tottenham, where it was converted into 'pudding' and sold as pig food.

A Borough of Stepney dust cart doing the rounds, *c.* 1920. The two dustmen are emptying bins into a cart that already looks as if it is filled to capacity.

Vehicle No. 13 of the Poplar Borough Council's Karrier Mechanical Street Cleaner.

A dustman emptying a bin into hand dust cart No. 15 for Poplar Borough Council, c. 1922. His dog waits patiently on the pavement. The large broom attached to the cart would have been used for sweeping up rubbish around the bins. Since refuse was emptied straight into the open-topped cart, which was then pushed along the streets, the dustman's job was particularly unpleasant and hazardous, with little regard for health and safety.

Dustmen working with a side-loading collection vehicle, 1949. An improvement on the previous picture, this vehicle was new and designed to make the dustman's work just a little easier. Another beneficial change is the protective gloves worn by the dustman.

Northumberland Wharf, 1940. The objects seen here are part of the 100 tons of scrap metal which was collected during July 1940, at Poplar, after Mayor Alderman J.H. Jones had made an appeal. Bedsteads and bathtubs make up the bulk of the scrap.

Salvaging rubber tyres at Northumberland Wharf, Poplar, 1940. These disused council dust carts contain salvaged rubber tyres. In the right foreground is an old tin trunk, a couple of birdcages, an iron bedstead and what looks like a brass fender.

Men sorting scrap, Northumberland Wharf, 1940. The appeal for scrap metal resulted in salvage which included a large number of tin baths, tin trunks and railings.

This undated picture shows three apparently happy refuse workers sorting out rubbish, including piles of newspapers, old tin baths and leather suitcases.

Official notices for salvage collection posted outside the town hall in the Bow Road, 1941. The notice for waste paper states: 'the waste paper collected during the first 18 months of the national salvage campaign would fill a continuous string of lorries stretching from London to Glasgow'. It concludes: 'The Council's contribution to this effort has been a good one – help us to continue the good work by letting the dustman have your old books – magazines – newspapers and any other material, which will assist the council's war effort.' The scrap metal poster states: 'The scrap metal collected during the last 18 months of the national salvage campaign is sufficient to provide steel for 10 destroyers, plus 10,000 tanks, plus 20 million 18 pounder shells'. It urges the public to provide as much as possible.

The waste paper corner at Northumberland Wharf.

Baling wastepaper into one-and-a-half hundredweight lots ready for despatch Northumberland Wharf, 1940.

A water cart used by Stepney Borough Council for cleaning. This street-cleaning vehicle is being inspected by the same unidentified visitor seen on p. 139.

Waste being discharged into barges at Northumberland Wharf, Blackwall, 1964.

Refuse disposal, 1949. Two workmen on a refuse barge on the Thames are levelling off the rubbish prior to hatching and covering for the trip down river. The man on the left is stripped to the waist, and the second man is not wearing any protective clothing either, but both seem unconcerned by the dangerous nature of their work.

A sewer-flushing gang in Glaucus Street, Bromley by Bow, 1950. These workers are dragging a length of sewer between manholes, as are the men in the bottom photograph. However, the winch in operation here is rather more substantial than the one below.

Dragging a length of sewer at Libra Road junction with Wright's Road, Poplar, 1950. A small bucket, called a mole, is pulled through on a wire rope by means of the winch on the sheer legs at the further manhole, and then dragged back, bringing deposit with it, which is emptied out into the wheelbarrow and disposed of elsewhere. After dragging it, the sewer is flushed with water from the tanker, seen in the background.

CHAPTER FOURTEEN

SCHOOLS & TRAINING CENTRES

The nursery crèche, 57 White Horse Road, Stepney, 1948. The nursery was opened after the Second World War by the Anglo USA relief fund, when Miss Olive, in the dark uniform, was appointed matron. It was taken over by Stepney Borough Council, and then on 5 July 1948 came under the control of the London County Council.

The Technical Schools at the People's Palace, Mile End, 9 June 1888. In October 1887 the Queen's Hall was opened as a free public library and reading room. By the generousity of the Drapers' Company, the old Bancroft School building in the rear of the hall was converted into a Technical School during the erection of the permanent buildings for which the Drapers' Company contributed a sum of £20,000. The contempory buildings were fitted with spacious and well-equipped workshops. Subjects taught included carpentry and joinery, hand-rail and staircase work, cabinetmaking, plumbing, engineering, etching and boot and shoe making. Chemical and physical laboratories and a school of art were also attached to the buildings. Over 900 students enrolled in the various evening classes within the first few months, which included tuition in shorthand, French, German and book-keeping. There were also classes particularly for young women in such subjects as dressmaking, millinery, plain needlework, cooking and housewifery.

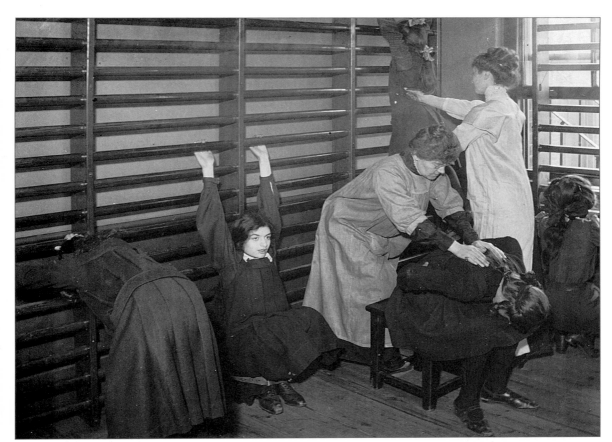

Gym class in the Central Foundation School, Spital Square, 1912. The school was originally founded as a charity school for boys and girls in Bishopsgate in about 1726, and moved to various locations within the parish until 1890 when a new girls' school was opened on the south side of Spital Square, Nos 33–5. In 1891 the boys' and girls' schools were brought together in a new foundation called the Central Foundation Schools of London. The girls' school later merged with Coborn School in Bow Road, which is now known as the Central Foundation School for Girls. When this picture was taken there were about 400 pupils at the school.

Opposite: Sgt Wigmore's boxing class at the Docklands Settlement, 1935. The settlement had a gymnasium where volunteers trained boys and girls. The National Association of Boys Clubs sent a number of helpers to instruct boys.

Miss Jones' dancing class, Docklands Settlement, 1935. The building, endowed by Lady Margaret Chateris, was originally opened in 1905 as a canteen for women workers, who had no place to go to during their breaks, except the local pubs. In 1923 it was converted into the Docklands Settlement, and provided the same facilities as other settlements in the East End. It was a thriving community centre with adult-education evening classes, mother and baby mornings, sewing classes, clubs for boys and girls and dance evenings for adults. Today the Settlement is home to the Island History Trust and the Quaystone Baptist church.

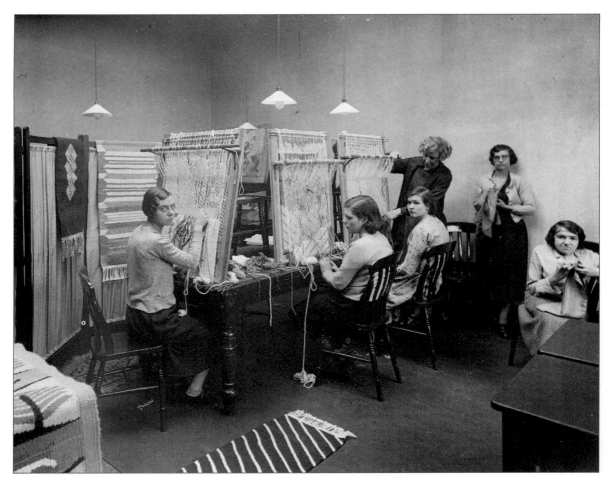

An occupational training centre for physically handicapped women, 45 Upper North Street. The centre, opened on 25 September 1936, was set up by the Council for the Promotion for Occupational Industries among the Physically Handicapped (CPOIPH). Initially, seventeen disabled women were trained to weave rugs and to embroider. The centre was the only one in London to open every day in the week and the experiment was regarded with a great deal of interest, for from very humble beginnings three years earlier in Devon's Road, it had made remarkable progress in Poplar.

At the end of 1933 the CPOIPH had opened a training centre for physically handicapped men and women in a room lent by Mr Kelly at the Devon's Road Mission. The numbers increased to such an extent that the men's class had to be separated and were held at St Leonard's church hall, Bromley by Bow. In 1936 it was decided to open a new centre for women in Poplar and a room was rented at 45 Upper North Street. The women made embroidered writing and needlework cases, baby rugs produced on the handlooms, men's ties, scarves etc. The number of cases helped during the following year was about 930, of whom 200 were being taught in their own homes. Those who were so physically handicapped that they could not leave their homes were visited by the teachers.

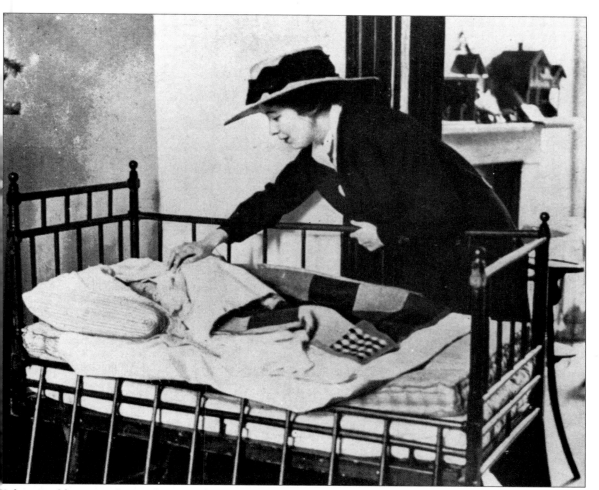

Sylvia Pankhurst at the Mother's Arms, 438 Old Ford Road. In April 1915, Sylvia Pankhurst, who lived at 400 Old Ford Road, which was the headquarters of the East London Federation of the Suffragettes, took over a disused pub, commonly known as the Gunmakers' Arms, which stood on the corner of St Stephen's Road and Old Ford Road almost opposite Gunmakers Lane. Here she opened a mother and baby clinic, a crèche for working mothers and a Montessori school. The clinic was staffed by two doctors, Alice Johnson and Barabra Tchaykovsky, a London County Council school doctor, and Nurse Maud Hebbes, who was later to become the first nurse at the Marie Stopes Birth Control Clinic. The crèche, run by Lucy Burgis, a trained nurse, attracted a great deal of public support and received grants from the Corporation of London and the Ministry of Health and Education. The Montessori school, organized by Muriel Matters, was one of the first to be opened in Britain. The project provided vital aid to women and children in Bow during the desperate years of the First World War, when many East End families were left to fend for themselves, with their men away from home and with no means of earning a living.

ACKNOWLEDGEMENTS

We are grateful to the following people and organizations:

A.A. Leech, Mrs Collins, A.S. Ramsey, Mrs P.M. Hood, Mrs V. Howard, Mr H. Willmott, Mr A.J. Moody, Mr D.R. Smith, Mrs R. Weller, Mr Stanley, Anthony Blake, William Whiffin, W.V. Stark, R.S. Magowan, Central Foundation School, Docklands Settlement, *Daily Sketch*, Sports and General Press Agency, *Planet News*, Halifax Photos, John Topham Picture Library, *East London Advertiser*, Salvation Army International Heritage Centre, Philip Mernick, Museum of London, Museum in Docklands, *Illustrated London News*.

HRH The Duchess of Kent paying an informal visit to the Bethnal Green Day Nursery, Somerford Street, *c.* 1935. She was received by Sir Percy Harris MP, the Mayor and Mayoress of Bethnal Green and Miss E.J. Marshall (Hon. Secretary).